We Oughta Be In Pictures . . .

Julia Willis

ALAMO SQUARE PRESS
San Francisco

Special thanks to Ben Eakin of Banned Books,
who designed this book, set the type
and had originally hoped to publish it.

Library of Congress Catalog Card Number: 92-075557
ISBN: 09624751-8-1

10 9 8 7 6 5 4 3 2 1

For Jennifer, Libba, and all my friends who do the characters, play the music, and entertain me

Contents

We Oughta Be In Pictures

As Tough As Comedy

"Mrs. Robinson, do you think we could say a few words to each other first this time?"
—The Graduate

Here's a nice long introduction, which will be followed by two comic lesbian screenplays. Now normally I hate reading introductory remarks, because they don't make sense unless you've already read the book. I promise this is not going to be that sort of dry commentary—some of it's funny, some of it's trashy, and a little bit here and there is even informative (hmm—I could probably say the same thing about the screenplays, or myself). Unless you have a good working knowledge of the lesbian in mainstream films, and you're acquainted with the more peculiar terms used in screenplays, I hope you'll take a few minutes to browse through these sections just to get your bearings. Then you can jump right into the screenplays with both feet (gee, I love that toenail polish you're wearing).

A small disclaimer: The characters portrayed in these filmscripts are entirely fictitious, and any resemblance to a lesbian you know, whether she's living or dead or just getting over a really nasty breakup, is purely coincidental. In addition, it must be stated that said filmscripts are intended solely for the purpose of entertainment; therefore, any suggestion that they must contain scenes of parental or societal disapproval (ie., Mother discovers child is gay and throws up in sink, ex-husband sues lesbian mother for custody and in court judge acts downright squeamish, neighbor belongs to Klan and burns cross on front lawn,) or should include those predictable moments of tender tolerance (woman comes out to best friend while walking on beach), or any implication that they don't take life seriously enough, shall be construed as misuse of the material. Repeat offenders will be told in no uncertain terms what to do if they can't take

1

a joke. I mean, really, girls. We got to remember a good laugh is next to Goddessliness.

Which reminds me of an old story: one time Tallulah Bankhead was lying on her deathbed (dying, naturally) and someone holding her hand said, "It's tough, isn't it?"

"Yes, darling," she replied, "but not as tough as comedy."

Come to think of it, maybe that wasn't Tallulah who said that, but she would certainly have known what it meant. And I hope you do, too.

A Sweet Story

"I remember every detail. The Germans wore gray. You wore blue."
— Casablanca

My first memory, and I mean my *very* first, is of being carried out of a car in wintertime and into a beautiful warm room with tall, gilded standing columns, floor-length drapes, a plush red carpet, a long counter stacked with small brightly colored boxes, and a mysterious glass cage full of little white exploding flowers. Then I was taken behind the counter, up a strange winding staircase, and into a tiny room crowded with whirring machinery and big spinning wheels. And as my daddy held me up to a window no larger than my baby head, I saw that the white light pouring out of one machine was piercing the dark void and throwing colorful dancing images on the far wall of a long room peopled by the human shadows of a crowd stirring and rustling below, while a sound box on the wall above me blared loud voices and music. I could recognize that box as similar to other sound boxes I'd seen and heard before, in the car and in the living room at home, but there was nothing in my short past to compare those dancing images to. This was some new and wonderful magic. It was also a movie I was watching from the projection booth of the Washington Theater where my daddy worked as a projectionist in a small Carolina town in the fifties. I was lucky enough to be in that last generation of children who had the glory of cinema implanted in their collective consciousness before television invaded every American home and made the word "entertainment" synonymous with "couch potato."

There *was* wonderful magic in the sizzling marquee, the palatial lobby, the sugary concession stand, and the torn leather folding seat in a room with pale orange art deco torches along the side walls and sticky cola syrup on the cool concrete floor. Even now, in spite of television and home video, there still is. It seems a curious thing that you can fill up a place with total strangers, turn out the lights, and expect them to behave civilly toward one another, but amazingly (if you don't count the balcony), you usually can. This is because that roomful of people isn't actually there — their bodies remain while their spirits disappear into that world on the screen and don't come back until the feature's over and the end credits are running. In the case of very good movies, or very frail psyches, a chosen few may never come back at all. (Like my cousin Becky, who sat through "Gone With the Wind" forty-seven times in twenty-eight days and then tried to raise an army to take back Richmond. I have to admit she did look real good in her uniform.) So we're dealing with a very powerful medium here, one that's firmly ingrained in our natures and quite capable of changing our lives forever. I mean, look at me. Ever since that night so long ago in the Washington Theater, I know I've never been the same.

Why Hollywood is Not My Kind of Town

"The last one I wrote was about Okies in the dust bowl. You'd never know because, when it reached the screen, the whole thing played on a torpedo boat."

—Sunset Boulevard

Wasn't that a sweet story? Most of it's even true. I'm sorry to say I can't tell you exactly what movie was playing that night, but I will bet you dollars to dildos that whatever it was, it was *not* a lesbian movie. And I can declare with some certainty there was not a single lesbian character in it. Why? Well, for one thing, I'm given to understand the Washington Theater, being a "B" picture moviehouse, tended to book the kind of action/adventure movies that then and now are rigidly heterosexual in content. (The men fight and the women fall down and sprain their ankles.) As for another reason, let's return to those thrilling days of yesteryear (1927) when "Lone Censor" Will Hays, who was hired by the studios to make them more presentable to Middle America, first introduced his list of what could and could not be expressed, implied, or even suggested onscreen. "Any and all references to sexual perversion" was right up there alongside nudity, drug trafficking, and ridiculing the clergy. As late as the fifties, a revised Production Code still banned allusions to venereal disease and the aforementioned business of "sexual perversion" (the quotation marks are mine—the phrasing, needless to say, is not). Add to this the studios' habit of adding a morality clause (which in essence said "if you get caught, it's your ass") to every actor's contract, and you have forty years of movie-making denying our existence being written, acted, and directed by a large number of talented men and women in their proverbial closets. So it's no great wonder that, in a country whose truths and myths have proliferated into gospel at the neighborhood Bijou for four generations, society is having quite a time incorporating us into its philosophical reality: no one was gay in the movies; therefore, how can anyone be gay?

Where to Find Dykes in the Movies

"But Your Majesty, you cannot die an old maid."
"I have no intention to, Chancellor — I shall die a bachelor."
—Queen Christina

This is not to say the lesbian *never* made it to the big screen, but her appearances were few and far between, and the context was rarely flattering. As a youth I may have been grateful just to *see* a lesbian scene in a major motion picture, no matter how ghastly the circumstances, but then I was thrilled the first time I ran across THE WELL OF LONELINESS in a Salvation Army bookstore, too. Now I'm a lot pickier. Anyway, in case this is all fairly new to you (bless your heart!), or even if it's not, here's my own selective rundown on sixty-odd movies and their lesbian themes and/or contents (1927–1992).

Before the rigid Production Code took effect, or in early foreign films, lesbians were occasionally introduced in relatively non-judgmental ways. In "Wings" (1927) the casual camera glances in passing at a couple of women in tailored suits holding hands and drinking champagne in a Parisian cafe. "Pandora's Box" (1928 — German) features a countess in love with Lulu (marvelous Louise Brooks); said countess isn't very subtle in her approach, but Lulu seems to have this effect on everyone she meets. (In this case, there was less of a problem with the role than with the homophobic actress playing the role—she refused to do her seductive scenes with Louise, and the director had to let her play them to him and the camera instead.) "Maedchen In Uniform" (1931 — German) is the touching story of a young girl in a repressive school in love with her teacher. And in "Morocco" (1930), a bold Marlene Dietrich (though she falls for a young, androgynous Gary Cooper later) walks into a club audience in her tux and tails and kisses a young woman on the mouth, eliciting surprise and delighted giggles but no shocked gasps from onlookers.

When the Code taboos of the thirties began to make their presence felt, lesbian characters almost disappeared. The mere suggestion that throughout history lesbians have existed was not a topic for discussion. Only Garbo, as "Queen Christina" (1933), could have gotten away with dressing in men's clothes, kissing and fawning over her favorite lady of the court, declaring to remain a bachelor. Even so, the script blames her abdication on her love for a purely fabricated Spanish ambassador (played by John Gilbert, who in real life begged Garbo to marry him when she insisted she simply wanted to be his friend—poor John obviously didn't get it). Lillian Hellman's play, "The Children's Hour," was first filmed in 1936, but the title was changed to "These Three" and the lesbian theme was dropped completely. The rumored affair was between Karen and her

Julia Willis

doctor boyfriend, instead of Karen and Martha, and hints of jealousy pitted the two women against each other. Makes you wonder why they even bothered to shoot it, but then Hellman always insisted it wasn't *really* about lesbians. (Sure, Lillian, we see, we understand.) Also in the thirties Katharine Hepburn went drag (and looked great—one critic said she looked better as a boy than as a girl) in "Sylvia Scarlett" (1936) and was kissed by a woman who thought she was a charming lad, but though many of us find this movie appealing in an odd sort of way, you can't exactly call it lesbian. A sleazy camp classic (along the lines of "Reefer Madness") with minor lesbian characters is "Sex Madness" (also known as "They Must Be Told!") (1934), in which one secretary in the ever-popular tailored suit makes overtures to another secretary in a frilly blouse, taking her to a burlesque show to watch girls in skimpy costumes dancing with barbells and inviting her home ("Want to stay at my place tonight?"). Pretty weird, but their appearance is all too brief; most of the movie is about boys and girls and syphilis.

In the forties, fifties, and early sixties, things only grew worse. The lesbians were so subtly concealed in the guise of (a) cold, spinster types, (b) broad butches, or (c) confused adolescents, that unless you were looking real hard for them (the way I was) I doubt you'd have gotten the message at all:

(a) Mrs. Danvers in "Rebecca" (1940) has an "unnatural" attachment to her dead mistress; the imperious woman friend of a young girl's dead mother who returns to haunt the old mansion on the cliff in "The Uninvited" (1944) is plainly "devoted" to her memory. Kim Stanley as "The Goddess" (1958) has a nurse who is obviously in love with her, as is Melina Mercouri's faithful servant in "Phaedra" (1962). There's something more than just "The Haunting" (1963) going on between Julie Harris and Claire Bloom, but it's achingly unrequited. Even as late as 1964, Tennessee Williams' "Night of the Iguana" uses a strangely hysterical woman as a traveling companion for young Sue Lyons.

(b) Emma (Mercedes McCambridge) in "Johnny Guitar" (1954) is so obsessed by Vienna (Joan Crawford) that the sexual tension between them leads to a good old Western shoot-out. "Walk on the Wild Side" (1962) features Barbara Stanwyck as one tough madam in a New Orleans brothel who has quite a thing for one of her girls. Mercedes McCambridge makes another appearance (this one a frightening cameo) as a sadistic leather dyke who enjoys watching Janet Leigh being terrorized in "Touch of Evil" (1958), and in "Requiem For a Heavyweight" (1962) a character named "Ma" is so butch that at first it was hard for *me* to tell she was a woman—and honey, that's butch.

(c) As for the girls in love with older women, we have "The Unfinished Dance" (1947), in which young dancer Margaret O'Brien is madly infatuated with ballet star Cyd Charisse, "Kathy O'" (1958), the story of an unhappy child star played by Patty McCormack who confesses her love of journalist Jan Sterling and runs away from home to be with her, and numerous other tomboy movies that always shift abruptly in the third act and end with the girl in a pink dress going to the prom. Only in "Member of the Wedding" (1952) does young Frankie, after much soul-searching and torment, find happiness of a sort with the girl next door.

If these movies sound curiously depressing, you ain't seen nothing yet. It almost makes you want to stick with pure cinema like "Tarzan and the Amazons" (1945), a fine example of the Amazon women in headbands carrying spears genre—in this one the women *aren't* looking for men as husbands or slaves, they kill as many of the greedy male intruders as possible, and they let Tarzan and Boy go in peace after the Ape-Man returns their gold. Okay, it may sound a little silly—but after all these dreary, veiled lesbian characters, isn't it a welcome change?

Speaking of change, the remake of "The Children's Hour" (1962) did mark the beginning of a shift in the way lesbians were portrayed onscreen. They weren't much better, but they were more obvious. The old Code was gone, and restrictions were either loosened or lifted entirely. Possibly this happened in a last-ditch effort to drag people away from their television sets, but more likely it was a reflection of society's being more willing to address "dangerous" subjects heretofore unspeakable—you know, like civil rights and Tampax ads. So this time the original script of "The Children's Hour" was left intact, and Shirley MacLaine does admit to Audrey Hepburn she has loved her "the way they said." Unfortunately, she then proceeds to hang herself, so the fact that Audrey holds her head high walking away from the cemetery is not what you'd call a happy ending. I think it's what you'd call a "crumb" of understanding. Ah, well.

Where to Find Dykes in the Movies II: The Sequel

"Ah, what's Troy Donahue got that's so special?"
"Honey, you're the kind that'd never know."

—House of Women

I sometimes don't know which is worse—having *no* role models, or having role models so demeaning and/or disheartening they almost convince you you must be straight after all. And this was the transitional sixties in a nutshell. With few exceptions, the following stereotypes set the tone for cinematic lesbian images perpetrated upon the movie-going public (to say nothing of the movie-going lesbians) until well into the recent past. Take your pick: we have the slinky seductress (played as either mean bitch or free spirit, often involved in threesomes), the criminal element (frequently on

Julia Willis

drugs or in jail), the pitiful lonely misfit, the young lovers who just haven't found the right man yet, and the dysfunctional couple (one butch, one femme, no hope). And you think you have troubles. . . .

The seductresses: Jean Seberg is seduced and abandoned by another mental patient, a cruel and beautiful one, in "Lilith" (1964). Remember Candice Bergen *before* "Murphy Brown?" In "The Group" (1966), her screen debut, she plays Lakey, a brilliant sorority sister all the girls are mad about who marries a butch countess. (But collegiate seductress or not, you gotta hand it to her — the woman has style and makes no pretense of hiding her sexuality. Lakey could give Murphy a few lessons . . . .) "The Killing of Sister George" (1968 — British) begins with a good old-fashioned dysfunctional butch and femme, and ends with a bold seduction scene of Susannah York by another more slinky butch. Playing a nasty power game in "X, Y, and Zee" (1972 — British), Elizabeth Taylor overwhelms her husband's mistress (poor Susannah York again — she was so willing to play lesbian parts, it's a pity they were so awful). As the wife of Lenny Bruce ("Lenny" (1974)), voluptuous Valerie Perrine makes love with a woman while he watches. Two older women who try to appear as elegantly lascivious as possible and merely manage to look awful, Alexis Smith and Melina Mercouri do their worst in "Once Is Not Enough" (1974). An interesting lesbian in an African safari suit briefly takes on "Emmanuelle" (1974 — French) before announcing her fear of commitment in an otherwise conventional soft porn movie. Catherine Deneuve, queen of seductresses everywhere, stars in "The Hunger" (1983) as a vampire who seduces Susan Sarandon and drinks her blood. And Anais Nin revels in her passionate attraction to the femme fatale June ("Henry and June" (1990)) before turning her attention to Henry.

Women on the fringe: A prison butch (and you can tell she's the butch because she's the only woman in the cell block in coveralls) draws a beard on another prisoner's picture of Troy Donahue and gets ten days in solitary — she serves as comic relief in "House of Women" (1962). Frank Sinatra as detective "Tony Rome" (1967) questions a stripper who goes back to her trailer park to fight and make up with her large alcoholic lover. (Frank smirks at the sight of them together. More comic relief. Ha ha.) "The Legend of Lylah Clare" (1968) plot is fairly confusing, but it seems that Lylah (Kim Novak) kills her female lover dressed in drag and then throws herself down the stairs. There's another quiet older lesbian skulking around the mansion, too. (No comic relief there.) Two other unpleasant mystery-thrillers using dull, mopey, or unbelievably psycho lesbians are "In the Glitter Palace" (1977 TV movie) and "Windows" (1980). "Liquid Sky" (1983) is low-budget lesbian punk, having something to do with heroin and alien murders, so no one's especially nice, though Anne Carlisle playing both the lesbian punk *and* a gay male model is rather engaging. By the mid-eighties, we have our choice of women's prison movies: either "Turning to Stone" (1985 — Canadian), which takes itself too seriously and includes one lesbian who has her "twisted" way with newcomers (and several other dykes who range from sympathetic butch to jealousy-crazed attacker), or "Reform School Girls" (1986), which doesn't take itself a bit seriously and includes a leather dyke (Wendy O. Williams) who has *her* "twisted" way with newcomers, etc. (don't you love variety?). And "Black Widow" (1986) is a mild attempt to create a lesbian undercurrent, with frumpy investigator Debra Winger obsessed by killer Theresa Russell—but that kiss is pure slinky seductress.

Poor, poor thing: All the pitiful misfit lesbian roles I know are so similar it would be tedious to discuss each one individually (true—repetitive, predictable roles *is* what we're dealing with here, but these are almost word for word—you could phone them in), so I'll just list them and comment on the slight variations that occur (much like mutations in nature). The prototype is "Rachel, Rachel" (1968), in which Estelle Parsons is a fellow teacher of Joanne Woodward's Rachel. Their loneliness nearly brings them together, but Rachel narrowly escapes her fate, though Estelle begs for more. ("Begging" is the operative word in the pitiful misfit scenario.) Following the pattern, we have "Sheila Levine Is Dead and Living in New York" (1975) (the upstairs neighbor begs Sheila), "Girlfriends" (1978) (Amy Wright, as a temporary roommate, begs Melanie Mayron of "Thirty—Something"), "The Rose" (1979) (Bette Midler has her hair washed by a loving fan who begs), "The Bell Jar" (1979) (a fellow mental patient begs the Sylvia Plath character and upon rejection commits suicide), and "Silkwood" (1983) (Cher is adorable as the roommate Dolly who never quite begs Meryl, but hangs around looking mighty lonely—and this is about as good as it gets with the pitiful misfit).

A couple of young lover movies which we consider lesbian movies (and which we watch over and over, grateful for the sex scenes) are "Therese And Isabelle" (1968) and "Personal Best" (1982). But am I the only one who's noticed that the lesbianism in both is treated as a phase girls grow out of and remember wistfully or fondly (like any first love) while riding or running into the sunset with a boy? Maybe I am.

Misery loves company: If lesbian couples really got along as badly as they generally appear to when they show up onscreen, we would indeed be better off married (and not to each other—which seems to be the underlying message of these dismal forays into the shadowy world of women alone together). Yeah, right. Well, let's start with "The Fox" (1968). I'll never forget this movie, because I saw it with the woman I loved—we were double-dating guys from our summer stock company at the time (but that's another movie).

Sandy Dennis bakes muffins, while Anne Heywood is stuck with all the heavy outside work until she finally finds a man to do it for her and Sandy gets hit by a tree. I personally see "The Fox" as a treatise on the dangers of role-playing. And I guess I could say the same for "The Killing of Sister George," which is well acted by Beryl Reid and good old Susannah but oh, it is *so* sad. (How many dysfunctional couples does it take to change a light bulb? None — they'd just as soon sit in the dark and feel sorry for themselves.) "To Forget Venice" (1979 — Italian) looks promising at first, with a gay male couple and a lesbian couple visiting their famous relative in the country, but what we get is a good look at the workings of the male relationship and a better look at the women's breasts. And one of the women is *so* sad. Liv Ullman, in "Richard's Things" (1980 — British), is a widow who has an affair with her dead husband's mistress. She's too paranoid to enjoy it, as well as being *so* sad. Mariette Hartley, in "My Two Loves" (1986) (with a script co-credited to Rita Mae Brown — this was before she began writing with her cat), is another widow. *She* has an affair with Lynn Redgrave, who plays a lesbian licking her chops with about as much subtlety as a cat stalking a canary (on second thought, maybe Rita Mae's cat did help her with this one). This good widow also becomes paranoid and runs off to her therapist, leaving poor Lynn *so* sad (what else is new?). With Donna Deitch directing and Oprah Winfrey along, "The Women of Brewster Place" (1989 TV movie) attempts to present a lesbian couple trying to be happy, but it doesn't really, and they aren't really, and after a fight, the one who wears dresses storms out alone, is raped, and then kills a wino, leading us to believe the moral was "never go out without your butch." I'm told what transpires in the novel is even worse, but still — it isn't that I'm demanding an end to all scenes where bad things happen to good lesbians, I just think it's time to demand a balance.

On a brighter note, since Stonewall there does seem to be a tiny trend toward presenting lesbians in a more positive light. This occurs about as often as Rita Mae's cat does book signings, but it can happen. Here are a few examples of lesbian characterizations I can watch without wincing: "Five Easy Pieces" (1970), with Helena Kallianiotes as a wonderful lesbian hitchhiker complaining about garbage; "Outrageous!" (1977 — Canadian), with Helen Shaver (pre-"Desert Hearts") as half of a caring lesbian couple who take care of the drag queen's schizophrenic friend; "A Question of Love" (1978 TV movie), which allows Gena Rowlands and Jane Alexander to be good mothers and act about as normal as two lesbians can without touching on camera; "A Different Story" (1978 TV movie), a pretty good role for Meg Foster (made before CBS called her "too dykey" for "Cagney and Lacey" and dropped her after the first season) —

but still a pity she and the faggot get married at the end; "Manhattan" (1979), where Meryl Streep does her best playing a lesbian ex-wife of Woody Allen, though she never quite convinces me— maybe she needed a wig, or an accent; "Lianna" (1983), a genuinely believable story of a woman who finds herself through the love of another woman, even if their relationship doesn't work out (now that sounds a bit more familiar, doesn't it, girls?); "The Color Purple" (1985), another instance of a woman discovering her own strength in the arms of a blues mama (and Whoopi Goldberg is so persuasive in the part you can bet hell will freeze over before she ever does anything like it again); "Desert Hearts" (1986), what many women consider to be the best thing to come along since sliced bread, so I have to acknowledge their feelings (although frankly, I'm sick and tired of going to parties that break up early because all but three of us are hovering around the VCR watching that scene in the motel room for the umpteenth time—there, I said it, and I'm glad); "I've Heard the Mermaids Singing" (1987—Canadian), whose story introduces the lesbianism as personally intriguing to the narrator and yet charmingly incidental; "Waiting For the Moon" (1987— PBS), showing Gertrude and Alice in a sincere and loving light (but which I would have enjoyed better if the characters or the actresses had more closely resembled the real Gertrude and Alice); "Oranges Are Not the Only Fruit" (1989—British—BBC), a faithful adaptation of the book, the story of a girl holding fast to her love and her convictions, fascinating if you can manage to sit through the fundamentalism; and "Portrait of a Marriage" (1992—British—BBC), the story of Vita Sackville-West and Violet Trefusis's all-too-brief affair which nevertheless had some dandy passionate moments.

But let us not imagine for an instant that the worst is over. For every baby step forward we take, Hollywood is just as apt to take a giant leap backward. Maybe in "Casablanca" a kiss was just a kiss, but according to Fannie Flagg, a kiss in her movie "Fried Green Tomatoes" (1991) would have been "political." So even though we know what was going on between Ruth and Idgie, America would rather pretend not to notice. And while that's just the sort of attitude that keeps lesbians abysmally low on the visibility scale, a movie like "Basic Instinct" (1992) turns visibility on its head with one easy three-million-dollar script that splashes lesbian-psycho-icepick-killers across the screen like so much high-concept garbage.

Of course, all these remarks are strictly my own opinions, of which I have a wide assortment for every occasion. I'm sure your list of rotten and favorite lesbian movies would be similar to mine in some respects and different in others. What I think we can agree on is that the movie industry's concept of lesbianism has by and large been distorted, depressing, and generally not something you'd want to take your best girl to on a Saturday night. Count 'em: how

Julia Willis

many decent lesbian characters have we got on our lists? Perhaps a dozen, in these many years? I suppose some people may call this progress, but I call it ridiculous.

A VCR, a Desert Island, and Me

"Okay, sister, but my idea of love is that love isn't ashamed of nothing."
                                                                    —The Women

As I say, we all have our own preferences, but putting together this dyke tally has made me realize how little I care for practically every lesbian movie known to woman. Although I once devoured them with the voracity of a starving animal (which only goes to show if you're desperate enough, you'll watch anything), and even now I continue to track them down and examine them like rare fossils, I don't number them among my favorite movies — you know, the ten I'd take with my honey and my VCR to the desert island. I base the movies I love not on raw lesbian content, but on an overall completeness, a harmony of script, look, pace, and chemistry — on their ability to capture me in the opening frames and not let me go until the final fadeout. It also helps if (a) they use powerful women like Garbo, Hepburn, Stanwyck, Crawford, Bette Davis — and their modern equivalents, such as they are, (b) the misogyny is kept to the barest minimum, and (c) their stories are of women being brave and/ or independent together, whether it be in wartime ("Keep Your Powder Dry," "Cry Havoc," "So Proudly We Hail," "Tender Comrade"), on the wicked stage ("Stage Door," "Dance, Girl, Dance," "Ziegfeld Girl"), fighting crime ("Marked Woman," "Three on a Match," "The Company She Keeps") surviving without dates ("The Women," "Gentlemen Prefer Blondes," "Kansas City Bomber") or camping it up in nature ("Untamed Women," "Prehistoric Women," "Daughter of the Jungle"). And here's the ironic twist: to suck me in, a movie (besides working on all levels and succeeding in whatever it sets out to do) has to allow me to invent my own subtext to pretend the women characters are lesbians and/or in love with one another — and I've done that subconsciously with almost every movie I've ever seen and enjoyed. This is what happens when you live in a heterosexual society, and it all started many movies ago. . . .

Another Sweet Story

"Golly — sisters!"
                                                                    —The Parent Trap

Recently I rewatched Mary Martin in "Peter Pan" and remembered how puzzled I was as a child to learn at the end of the show that Peter was not going to disclose she was really a woman. Shucks. I soon caught on to the idea that the final reels in life and in art were not necessarily going to make sense to me. So I learned to watch Doris Day in buckskin singing "My Secret Love" and to shrug it off when she married Wild Bill Hickok at the end. But nothing in life had prepared me at the age of eight for Kim Novak in "Jeanne Eagels," the story of a woman who refuses to marry and, after working carnivals as a sleazy dancer, makes her way to New York, becomes a great actress with the help of Agnes Moorehead and, still feeling unfulfilled, drinks and drugs herself into an early grave.

Now the big girls in my neighborhood were nothing like Kim Novak, and they certainly didn't have that kind of cleavage. Neither did my mother, who didn't allow me to see grown-up movies like this. It was only sheer luck (and fate?) that caused it to rain on Bobby Bowen's outdoor birthday party that day, so that his mother in a panic and a wild burst of inspiration took the ten of us down to the Joy and dropped us off to see whatever was playing, anything to keep our muddy little saddle shoes off her furniture. Most of the kids ran up and down the aisles and threw Necco wafers at each other, while I sat with my eyes glued to the screen and my stomach doing flip-flops. Any remaining doubts as to my sexuality were wiped away as surely as that summer shower washed off Bobby Bowen's flagstone patio. I was reborn, hallelujah, and I walked around in a daze for weeks. And this in response to a movie that barely hinted at the fact that Jeanne Eagels was not your average straight woman (which indeed the real Jeanne Eagels was not). What might I have done if Bobby's mother in a different decade had dropped us off at "Desert Hearts?" I don't know—but at that age, in that time, all I needed was Kim Novak to confirm who I was and what I was going to be when I grew up. Bless you, Kim. (And bless you, too, Hayley Mills, for tapping into another hidden archetype of mine—the one of the loving soulmate "sisters" separated at birth and reunited at camp—with "The Parent Trap.")

Thus it was that long before I ever found lesbians in books, in history, in art (let alone in real life), I found love at the movies.

The Cold Hard Facts

"Scream, Ann — scream for your life!"

—King Kong

Be that as it may, no matter what I found and how pleasant it was, I felt what I did in spite of what Hollywood told me to feel—for we are lesbians not because society puts the idea in our heads and then proceeds to reinforce this idea with a barrage of media images that sell sex along with toothpaste, cars, and low cholesterol margarine, but because we can't be true to ourselves and be anything else. You'd think the philosophy of being oneself would fit right in with America's love of rugged individualism, but alas—rugged individualism not only doesn't apply to women, it's actu-

Julia Willis

ally a myth the boys use as a cover for the real bottom line that's built this nation—namely, the profit motive. And Hollywood is the epitome of the profit motive in action, now more so than ever.

Let me put it this way: Hollywood doesn't change, and neither will its movies. In these days of the blockbuster, 95% of the time on multiplex screens across the country the boy characters are still doing things while the girl characters in tight clothes watch breathlessly. The best concessions made to the women's movement are that the girl characters in tight clothes watching breathlessly now have these supposed offcamera professions like lawyer or neurosurgeon, and they sprain their ankles while running from the villains 33% less. Occasionally there will be a bland attempt to mollify one minority or another with a "daring" picture that will prove to be controversial in Georgia (where everything, including original thought, continues to be controversial). Rule of thumb: one or two sympathetic minor lesbian characters a year is the quota. Our diet still consists mainly of those crumbs of understanding they were tossing us back in the sixties. All the little dykes growing up in my hometown are falling in love at the movies the very same way I did, only without Kim Novak.

The Warm Soft Fantasies
"I don't think I would. I'm not afraid, Mother. I'm not afraid."
— Now Voyager

After a brief period in the seventies, when our idealism reached new heights and we believed anything was possible and gay prosperity was just around the corner (a time when I was *sure* Mary and Rhoda on "The Mary Tyler Moore Show" were going to become a couple—I mean, it was the only reasonable conclusion), we realized our books, our music, our arts were not going to be done correctly by anyone but us. It's like my mother always used to say—"If you want anything done right, do it yourself." No, wait a minute—that was my great-grandmother who said that. It was my mother who said—"Just shit, and let the hogs eat it." Or was that my grandmother? Oh, yes, it was. Then what did my mother say? Oh, that's right. Mother always said—"Just don't tell your father." Well, they all had the right idea. So we pitched in and did it. The body of gay and lesbian literature produced in the past twenty years is extraordinary. Women's music has come out of the woods and moved into the mainstream. The realms of art and photography have followed suit. And gay and lesbian film and video production companies have been springing up hither and yon, and we are in fact creating our own films and videos at a modest but steady clip.

Yes, there is hope! Yes, you can rent or buy these works through gay and lesbian distributors, or you can see them at gay and lesbian film festivals in most major cities. Unfortunately, the lesbian work routinely makes up 25% or less of the schedule at festivals (and this includes showings of mainstream films such as the previously mentioned "The Legend of Lylah Clare" and "Oranges Are Not the Only Fruit"), and this occurs for several reasons: (a) because boys continue to be more visible; (b) because boys have access to financing to produce feature-length films; and (c) because boys know how to entertain each other. It's taken the AIDS epidemic to politicize gay men, whereas most lesbians, with their strict feminist perspective, have been so political from the word "go" that sometimes (especially up North) it's like pulling eye teeth to get the girls to enjoy themselves for a whole evening without feeling guilty. So not only is there less representation of lesbians at these screenings due to said visibility and/or money issues, but chances are what there is will tend to be of a more enlightening nature. Short documentaries on women of color in early jazz, narrative clips about mothers and daughters, dance pieces that represent the death of the Amazon rain forest or the rebirth of the goddess, and video art of a woman shouting "I will not go, and you cannot make me!" Now I'm not saying this isn't fine stuff—it's great, and it's important, and it needs to be done. But we haven't exactly rushed to take up the slack Hollywood has handed us when it comes to producing features with lesbians in major roles that are somewhat less educational and somewhat more just for fun.

We do, I'm happy to say, have "Two In Twenty" (a five-hour lesbian soap opera from Boston which falls into the category of good, clean, politically aware fun) and some funny short videos springing from the mind of Ingrid Wilhite. And there has recently come into being an interesting subgenre known as the lesbian erotic video. I'm not sure I can be a very good judge of it, since I rarely find myself attracted to women solely on the basis of looks (a character trait which my friends say has kept me out of all kinds of trouble). Lesbian erotica tends to expend most of its budget and its energy on nice-looking bodies that interact in beds and barns and whatnot, leaving a lot to be desired as far as acting, plot, theme, direction, and overall continuity are concerned. Scenes just plop right in without warning, and characters disappear halfway through with no explanation and never come back. (Not my cup of tea—I mean, even Kim Novak movies had plots.) But they're fun, because they're ours— we're making them with our own two hands. So to speak.

All right, let's fantasize for a minute. (No, not that sort of fantasy, even if we were discussing lesbian erotica. Can't you ever think about anything else?) What shall we do now? (Movies—we're talking about *movies*.) That is, what would you like to see next? (Oh, please. I would never do that in front of my readers, so don't even think about it.) Well, I know what I'd like to see.

Julia Willis

Two-way conversation with myself, since no one else seems to be taking me seriously:

"I know what I'd like to see."

"Oh? What's that?"

"I'd like to see women making their own feature-length movies."

"You mean with character and plot and all like that?"

"Yeah—all that good stuff."

"Some sex, too?"

"Yeah—some. Not gratuitous, of course."

"Oh no, never gratuitous."

"Well—hardly ever gratuitous. But real movies."

"Wow—that would be great, wouldn't it?"

"Yeah, it would."

"But I wonder how we'd go about it. It's awfully expensive, isn't it?"

"Well—that depends. . . ."

Fear of Finance

"Money isn't all, you know, Jett."
"Not when you got it."

—Giant

No one has ever said making movies is not difficult, both as a collaborative effort and a financial venture, though there are things that help to make it easier. They are:

(1) Being very organized.

(2) Not sleeping with the producer.

(3) Sleeping with the producer.

(4) Having lots of money.

Most of the women I know and have worked with are much more likely to be familiar with (1), (2), or (3) than (4), myself included. Women on the whole have spent far fewer generations in the workforce, making and handling large sums of money. Our mothers taught us how to scrimp and save and keep our pile of crumpled dollar bills hidden in a glass loafpan in the pantry, while our fathers taught our brothers how to say phrases like "sixty-five thousand, minimum." It's a changing world, but even so we continue to think of money as something real ("and with that four thousand, we can open another shelter"), while to the boys it's just an abstraction ("we must have another four hundred billion for defense, Senator"). For women artists like myself, who have never had any money to practice with, it's a particularly thorny dilemma. which you girls who are becoming queens of industry will have to help us with. Because the first thing we have to recognize is we are dealing with a medium that costs A Lot Of Money. (Do not panic—this is only a test.)

To give you some notion of what Hollywood with its boys and their abstractions spends on productions, a typical film's average cost per day is about $33,000. (Of course, this would include the caterer—and people are eating a lot more on the set these days, now that they've gotten all those drugs out of their systems.) And costs are rapidly rising. The movie which cost $9.3 million dollars to make in 1980 by 1989 was costing $23.5 million. You know how it is, a million here, a million there. (Actually, you don't know how it is, which is the point, which will be to your advantage in the long run. Honest.) Those costs keep right on escalating, rather like the national debt, and the boys keep right on acting like this is perfectly okay and normal.

Here's the pitch: the aspiring young boy-wonder filmmaker starts out in film school borrowing money from his parents' friends and works his way up to a three-picture deal at Paramount. His first independent feature (and his best, probably) is made on a shoestring for under half a million, the second (with studio backing) comes in at $7 million, and then first thing you know he's acting like Spike Lee, complaining that if he doesn't get his $18 million for his next picture he'll go over to Warner Brothers. So he gets it. And he continues to get it until his pictures lose more money than they make, and then he goes off to teach other aspiring young boy-wonder filmmakers.

This is how it presently works. Amazing, is it not? But don't worry. Just be aware there's a lot of abstract money being thrown around in the film world, and don't let that intimidate you, because in comparison, the amounts you and I need to make wonderful pictures will be miniscule—say, a mere hundred thousand (gasp-choke). Nothing to it. So let's get used to it, girls, it's show business.

"It's a Miracle"

"Faith is believing in things when common sense tells you not to."
—Miracle on 34th Street

What women have already learned (aren't they clever!) is that video is a financially reasonable and aesthetically sound alternative to film. It's also a lovely, accessible medium. Granted, there are some shots video will never do justice to. Externals, for instance, look too flat (and remind you of British television), and color is often a little grainy. So if you plan to shoot a fifteen-minute car chase sequence involving police cruisers, roadblocks, exploding oil trucks, and the obligatory pick-up piled high with crates of chickens that will be scattered all over the road like boxes of Post Toasties, you might want to go to film (and film school). The same goes for prolonged battle sequences with terrorists, aerial stunts, and establishing shots of lower Manhattan at sunset from the New Jersey side. Again this

Julia Willis

is to our advantage, since I can't say I know that many women who are yearning to glorify, in proper perspective and living color, either car chases or extreme violence. (And if we must have that shot of lower Manhattan, we can always go to stock film footage.) So video is definitely our salvation and our strength. Along with working from uncomplicated scripts (no car chases or explosions), keeping post-production costs to a minimum, and using actors who'll work for scale, it's video that's going to help us make the lesbian movies of tomorrow. And it's home video that will bring our movie palaces as close as the nearest VCR.

Obviously it's going to take more than what I'm casually throwing out here to turn any healthy young dyke into an aspiring video-maker. Someone else will have to write the definitive how-to book. This is a book meant to get the ball rolling and the minds attuning themselves to the possibilites inherent in the form. And the next step is to read a couple of lesbian screenplays of the near future (which I just happen to have here with me) and then imagine where we can go from there.

All You'll Need to Know About a Screenplay in Five Minutes
"Shut up and deal."

—The Apartment

Sit back, put your feet up on the seat in front of you, and prepare to enjoy "Once Upon A Dream" (lesbian erotica *with* plot and character) and "Amazon X" (a science fiction fantasy that may be only one small step away from reality).

If you've never read a screenplay before, try to think of it as a play that moves around more. (And please don't tell me you don't like to read plays. Personally I don't much care for prose, there's too much descriptive crap cluttering up the page, though I manage to muddle through it to get to the dialogue.) It's just a matter of getting used to the format and picturing the scenes as they take place. As you read, in your mind you can cast Jodie Foster and Holly Hunter in any parts you like, and you don't even have to pay them. This is the price of fame, and it's your gain. Or you can play all the parts yourself. Or you can invite your friends over and read it aloud. Together. (Wow—this could be bigger than softball!) And another nice thing about reading a screenplay is it's similar to running a film on your VCR: you can pause whenever you want to make popcorn or go to the bathroom.

NOW PLEASE NOTE: Usually screenplays are either shooting scripts OR reading scripts. In a shooting script (a script ready to be shot, or already shot) the scenes would be numbered, and you'd get a description of every camera shot. A reading script has almost none of that, because in the initial stages of production directors don't like writers to tell them what to shoot unless it's absolutely necessary to the telling of the story. They're funny that way; they like to make up the shots themselves; it's what they get paid for. Now the two screenplays in this book are what I would call "modified" reading scripts—primarily scenes with occasional camera shots thrown in. Strictly speaking, this is not proper form (girls, don't try this at home!), but I'm presenting them this way so that unfamiliar readers can get a sense of both reading and shooting formats and see how the camera language and other screenplay terms defined below may be used in context. In addition to these nuts and bolts of terminology, there are dozens of specific rules for abbreviation, punctuation, page layout, continuing scenes or speeches from one page to another, etc.—and if you want to study them thoroughly and correctly, get a good book on screenplay format.

Here then is a list of screenplay terms you might want to acquaint yourself with:

FADE IN: This is how you know the movie is starting.

EXT./INT., etc. Scene headings start each new scene and describe the new location using some or all of these elements:

> EXT./INT.—whether it's an exterior or interior set
>
> KITCHEN— the place
>
> DAY/NIGHT— the time
>
> CLOSE SHOT/MED. SHOT/LONG SHOT— the camera angle
>
> JANE— the camera subject

ESTABLISHING This appears in scene headings. Usually the camera will look at the outside of a location before going in, to "establish" where the place is.

P.O.V. An abbreviation of "point of view," it's used in headings and means shooting through the eyes of the person named (as in JANE'S P.O.V.). There's also REVERSE P.O.V., where after looking at someone from Jane's P.O.V., the camera switches over to the someone and looks back at Jane.

OVER THE SHOULDER and ANGLE ON Two more camera references found in headings. The camera is behind Jane, shooting "over her shoulder," or the camera "angle" was looking at the whole room and narrows its focus to shoot Jane (ANGLE ON JANE).

INSERT Also used in headings to show the camera focusing on a detail like a photograph, it's similar to a CLOSEUP.

STOCK FOOTAGE Old film shots of city skylines, waves breaking on the shore, elephants thundering across the veldt, etc.—you pay a fee and use it rather than shooting your own elephants.

b.g. An abbreviation of "background."

f.g. An abbreviation of "foreground."

O.S. An abbreviation of "off screen." It means you hear someone talking, but they're out of camera range.

---

18   Julia Willis

V.O. An abbreviation of "voice over," which is the character talking to herself, or could be a voice coming through a telephone, radio, or television (anything mechanical).

beat, (. . .), and (--) Various ways of pausing in the dialogue.

INTERCUT Means to go back and forth between two places, showing what's happening in both.

CUT TO:/DISSOLVE TO: A quick jump or a slower fade from one scene to the next. Only used for emphasis.

MATCH CUT/MATCH DISSOLVE Going from one scene showing an object (like a frying pan) to a scene showing the same or a similar "matching" object (another frying pan, or a grill) somewhere else.

FADE OUT. Time to gather up your loose gloves, knock over your popcorn cup, and go home.

Words and phrases that do just what they sound like they do include AD LIB, SERIES OF SHOTS, CREDITS or TITLES BEGIN or END, CONTINUED, MORE, BACK TO SCENE, SLOW MOTION, and FREEZE FRAME.

In addition to camera terms like P.O.V., ANGLE ON, and INSERT, you might run across self-explanatory terms like LONG SHOT (Jane is at a distance), FULL SHOT (Jane is closer, seen from head to toe), MED. SHOT (Jane is "medium" close, seen from the waist up), TWO SHOT (Jane and someone else, similar to MED. SHOT), CLOSE SHOT (just Jane's head and shoulders), and CLOSEUP (just Jane's face). Other camera movements you'll want to know are PAN (the camera goes left to right, or vice versa), DOLLY (the camera moves along with Jane, either handheld or on a track), and ZOOM (the camera goes in or out).

That's enough to get us started. So—nothing to it. Lights, camera, action—we're ready for you, Norma.

The Sweetest Story of All

"As you grow older, you'll find that the only things you regret are the things you didn't do."
                                                                    —Mildred Pierce

Hopefully, dear fellow movie lovers and lovers of women, this little discussion has helped put the cinematic lesbian past in perspective and the cinematic present in a realistic light, so we can now go on to invent our own cultural future by predicting and creating precisely what needs to come next.

See, I had this dream . . . well, I've had many dreams, and a few of them are nightmares, but most of them are wonderful. And some of them even come true. Twenty-five years ago, as I rifled through bookstores desperately seeking lesbian material, I dreamed one day gay people would have their own presses, their own newspapers and magazines, their own bookstores. As hard as I've hoped and believed in that, sometimes I still have to rub my eyes and pinch myself when I realize that dream has become a reality. Maybe you were dreaming then of women playing music or doing comedy or making their own erotic videos. Well, you've got it. Of course, you didn't get it by clicking the heels of your ruby slippers together; we've been working our asses off, both in the creation of these things and the support of them.

In every new beginning it's infinitely reassuring to hear a good witch Glenda ("Come out, come out") say, "You can do it. You've always had the power. You just had to find it out for yourself." First comes the fantasy, then comes the fact. So I'm asking you to imagine movies that reflect us as we really are—brave, funny, beautiful women—often noble, occasionally foolish, and forever prepared to leave the world better than we found it. Imagine them for the lesbians who'll come after us, our daughters in spirit. (And while you're at it, imagine movies where straight people are the minor characters for a change—gee, just like in everyday life—won't that be fun?) Just imagine all our comedies, our dramas, our adventures. . . .

Because they're already here, as Amazon X would say, "in our hearts."

Julia Willis
Boston, Massachusetts
October, 1992

Once Upon a Dream

FADE IN:

EXT. ROUTE SIX TO PROVINCETOWN - DAY - EXTREME LONG SHOT

A stark look at the dunes and the empty highway. As we HEAR the first movement of Mozart's "EINE KLEINE NACHTMUSIK":

BEGIN TITLES

On the far horizon a middle-aged Volvo comes into view and slowly approaches. When it finally reaches us and goes on, down the highway, the CAMERA FOLLOWS.

END TITLES

INT. LESLIE'S MOVING CAR/THE VOLVO

The MUSIC (now coming from the car RADIO) CONTINUES. JILL is riding to the Cape on a Sunday afternoon in early summer with her friends LESLIE and LAURA. They are all three in their late twenties to mid-thirties.

Leslie and Laura are in the front seat and Leslie is driving. They are a happy couple and have been together long enough to look somewhat alike and finish one another's sentences.

Jill is in the back seat by herself. Laura talked her into coming along on this trip, and now she is having second thoughts.

                    JILL
          (referring to the Mozart)
     Do we have to listen to this?

                    LESLIE
     Yes, Jill.

                    JILL
     Why?

                    LAURA
     Because it's lovely, that's why. Very romantic.

                    JILL
     You're kidding.

                    LESLIE
     No, she isn't.

                    JILL
     You two must've known each other in a previous life. Like in the eighteenth century.

Laura takes Leslie's hand and kisses it.

                    LAURA
     That's quite possible.

                    LESLIE
          (to Jill)
     Will you relax? Take a nap or something.

23

                          LAURA
Yeah, chill out.

                           JILL
Okay, okay.

Jill leans back and closes her eyes.

                        JILL (V.O.)
                 (meaning Laura and Leslie)
You've got nothing to be nervous about. You know who you're
sleeping with tonight. You guys have probably been sleeping together
for two hundred years.

                                              DISSOLVE TO:

EXT. A FORMAL GARDEN (JILL'S FANTASY) - DAY

(NOTE: This is the first in a series of fantasies. Ideally the DISSOLVE should
    always be accompanied by a HARP ARPEGGIO.)
The Mozart MUSIC continues. Laura and Leslie, in long dresses with low-cut
bodices, stroll hand-in-hand along a garden path. They stop. Laura raises
Leslie's hand to her lips and kisses it. Leslie places her hand on Laura's breast.
Laura breathes in sharply. They look longingly into one another's eyes.

                        LAURA (V.O.)
I *love* butter brickle.

                                               CUT TO:

INT. LESLIE'S MOVING CAR

Jill opens her eyes. She was only fantasizing Laura and Leslie in the garden.

                           JILL
Huh?

                          LAURA
Their butter brickle. Have you tried it?

                           JILL
Whose butter brickle?

                          LAURA
Poit's. The old drive-in. Up here on the right.
                 (beat; turning to Jill in the back seat)
Where have *you* been?

                           JILL
I was just thinking.

                         LESLIE
Uh-oh.

───

LAURA
Now this is a fun weekend -- no thinking allowed.

JILL
Yeah.
(still worrying)
Who's going to be there?

LAURA
At Poit's?

JILL
In P-Town.

LESLIE
Everybody.

LAURA
(to Leslie)
I think she wants specifics.

JILL
Yes, I do.

LESLIE
(fishing for names)
Oh -- Ann and Karen said they might be down.

JILL
They're a couple.

LESLIE
So?

LAURA
She only wants singles.

LESLIE
Give them a chance . . . maybe they'll break up.

JILL
Thanks.

LESLIE
I don't know who's going to be there, Jill. Just wait and see.

LAURA
Yes, just wait. There'll be hordes of fabulous single women lining the streets.

JILL
(leaning back; more to herself)
I think this was a mistake.

LAURA
(to Leslie)
We haven't passed it, have we?

                    LESLIE
Passed what?

                    LAURA
Poit's.

                    LESLIE
Oh. No.

                    JILL
I shouldn't have let you talk me into this.

                    LESLIE
                 (referring to Jill)
What is she mumbling about?

                    LAURA
She's psyching herself up to be miserable.

                    JILL
I just have to be realistic.
                 (talking herself into it)
No one can expect -- in just one night -- to find *real* true love --

                    LESLIE
                 (to Laura)
What's that flavor I like?

                    JILL
-- or great passion --

                    LAURA
Mocha chip?

                    JILL
-- or high adventure . . .

Jill trails off as a car passes them on the left. It's a bright red convertible driven by THE DREAMGIRL.

JILL'S P.O.V. - THE DREAMGIRL'S MOVING CAR

The Dreamgirl's car goes by in SLOW MOTION, while O.S. Laura and Leslie talk about ice cream.

                    LESLIE (O.S.)
That's it.

                    LAURA (O.S.)
Yeah . . . mocha chip.

                    LESLIE (O.S.)
MMMmmm -- delicious.

                    LAURA (O.S.)
MMMmmm -- now my mouth's watering.

LESLIE (O.S.)
Mine, too.

EXT. THE DREAMGIRL'S MOVING CAR - CLOSE SHOT - THE DREAMGIRL

This is also in SLOW MOTION. Her face is in profile. She's dressed all in white with a white scarf around her neck billowing out behind her. The effect created is that she is too perfect to be real. A BELL RINGS.

INT. LESLIE'S MOVING CAR

SLOW MOTION goes back to NORMAL SPEED, and the Dreamgirl and her car are gone in a flash.

JILL
(under her breath)
Oh my God.
(to Laura and Leslie)
Did you see that?

LAURA
What?

LESLIE
The Mustang?

LAURA
(seeing it ahead in the distance)
Oh, nice color.

JILL
No, no, the woman! The woman driving it!

LESLIE
No, missed her.

LAURA
What's wrong -- is she in trouble?

JILL
No, I am! I'm in love! Oh, follow that car!

Leslie makes a half -hearted effort, speeding up.

JILL
(continuing; pounding on the back of the front seat)
Can't you step on it? We're losing her.

LESLIE
I don't think we can catch her, Jill.

JILL
No -- we *have* to.

LAURA
She's going awfully fast.

Once Upon a Dream   27

                              JILL
Then go faster, faster!

                             LESLIE
                           (sarcastic)
**Why don't I just pull alongside and you can leap into her back
seat?**

                              JILL
                            (frantic)
Hurry, hurry! She's almost out of sight!
                            (praying)
**Oh, please don't let her turn off this road -- oh please, oh please,
oh please!**

                             LESLIE
This is ridiculous. I can't hope to go that fast.

                             LAURA
                     (as the car disappears)
Aah -- there she goes.

                              JILL
Oh, please, Leslie, we *have* to find her.

                             LAURA
                        (always helpful)
Maybe she'll stop at Poit's.

A SIREN is heard in the distance. Leslie looks in her rearview mirror.

                             LESLIE
Uh-oh.

Laura turns to look behind them.

                             LAURA
Uh-oh. Better pull over, honey.

Jill groans and leans back in her seat.

EXT. A PICNIC TABLE AT POIT'S

Laura and Leslie are sitting at a picnic table eating their ice cream cones. Jill
is pacing around them, looking for the Dreamgirl's car in the parking lot.

                             LESLIE
                       (shaking her head)
I still can't see why we got stopped and she didn't.

                             LAURA
He probably couldn't catch her.

                              JILL
                        (through looking)
Well, she's not here.

LAURA
Jill, don't you want to try the mocha chip?

JILL
I'm not hungry.
(beat: impatient)
Can't you finish those in the car?

LESLIE
(flatly)
No. Are you going to be this obnoxious all weekend?

JILL
I'm sorry.
(beat)
I'll pay the ticket.

LESLIE
That's not what I mean.

JILL
I'll stop being obnoxious just as soon as I find her.
(crosses her heart)
I promise.

LAURA
What if you can't find her?

JILL
Laura! Bite your tongue! I *have* to find her. She's going to be the love of my life!

Jill is practically shouting. She realizes she is beginning to attract attention and sits down at the other end of the table.

LAURA
I thought Andrea was the love of your life.

JILL
No. Not really.

LESLIE
What about Terry?

LAURA
Oh no, not Terry. They never had the right chemistry.

Laura and Leslie go on discussing AD LIB who could have been the love of Jill's life. Jill's mind begins to wander off on its own.

JILL
No, this is it . . . I just know it. I mean, I can hardly believe it's happening to me . . .

DISSOLVE TO:

EXT. A BEACH BY THE WATER'S EDGE (JILL'S FANTASY) - SUNSET

The Dreamgirl stands by the ocean, watching a beautiful sunset. She is wearing a white, diaphanous robe. The wind blows through her hair and the robe clings to her breasts.

The only SOUNDS are the gentle LAPPING of the waves and the CRIES of seagulls. She slips the robe off her shoulders, it drops to the sand, and she steps out of it. Her body glows pink in the light. She is an ocean goddess.

She turns to the camera and smiles. Then we SEE she is smiling at another WOMAN (not Jill) IN A BLACK ROBE. The woman approaches her and they embrace.

                                                                    CUT TO:

EXT. A PICNIC TABLE AT POIT'S - DAY

Jill sighs. Laura and Leslie are still talking about the loves of her life.

                              LAURA
        Oh, what *was* her name?

                              LESLIE
        Janet? Janis?

                              JILL
                         (to herself)
        Oh, even if she's not a dream, she must have someone. How could
        anyone so beautiful be single? . . .
                         (smiling)
        Besides me, of course.

Laura and Leslie are standing up, ready to go now.

                              LAURA
        Jill, who was that golf pro you knew in Dallas?

                              JILL
                         (making a face)
        Gail.

                              LESLIE
        Gail, that was it.

                              LAURA
                         (teasing Jill)
        Wasn't *she* the love of your life?

Jill gets up to leave with them.

                              JILL
        Yeah. For about fourteen hours.

                              LESLIE
        Short life.

Julia Willis

EXT. THE GUESTHOUSE IN P-TOWN - DAY - ESTABLISHING

The front of the guesthouse, with several of its rooms facing the parking lot. Leslie's car is parked in front of number seven, and it's empty. The Dreamgirl in her convertible drives by in the f.g. as we LOOK on.

INT. ROOM NUMBER SEVEN

Laura lies on one of the double beds in a seductive pose, looking toward the bathroom. Jill is sitting on the other bed nearest the door, obsessing about the Dreamgirl. Leslie comes out of the bathroom.

LESLIE

There're only two sets of towels.

LAURA

We'll share.

JILL

You think she turned off at Truro?

LAURA/LESLIE
(together)

No.

LESLIE

For the third time.

Leslie joins Laura on the bed.

JILL

How am I going to find her?

LAURA
(hinting)

I have a wonderful idea. Why don't you go and *look* for her?

LESLIE

That *is* a wonderful idea.

Jill gets up and goes to the door.

JILL

Okay, okay . . . a girl can always tell when she's not wanted.

LAURA/LESLIE
(together)

Bye.

Jill exits. We HEAR the door close behind her. Leslie puts her hand on Laura's thigh.

LESLIE

And can a girl tell when she's wanted?

LAURA

Always.

Once Upon a Dream

INTERCUT - EXT. COMMERCIAL STREET/INT. ROOM NUMBER SEVEN

BEGIN ON JILL

Jill walks down the street, looking for the Dreamgirl. Something in a shop window catches her eye. She looks at a scarf of luscious purple silk.

LAURA AND LESLIE

Leslie unbuttons Laura's purple shirt and cups her breast in her hand. They kiss.

JILL

Jill, walking, sees a woman who resembles the Dreamgirl from behind. The woman turns . . . it's not the Dreamgirl, just a woman sipping a fast food soda through a straw.

LAURA AND LESLIE

Laura plays with Leslie's nipple, touching and sucking it. They are both naked to the waist.

JILL

Jill stops in front of a bakery and looks at the display case filled with eclairs and pastries.

LAURA AND LESLIE

Laura and Leslie are naked. Leslie runs her hand over Laura's smooth belly and down the insides of her thighs.

JILL

Jill pauses in front of a bookstore window and reads the title of a steamy bestseller.

JILL (V.O.)

"HOT AND WET." A story of unbridled passion in the Amazon jungle.

LAURA AND LESLIE

A scene of unbridled passion between Laura and Leslie. Sweet, playful, deeply sensuous sex that we feel right down to our toes.

END ON JILL

Jill is still staring into the bookstore window.

JILL
(rereading the title)

"HOT AND WET."

Julia Willis

In the window reflection we SEE MARTHA standing behind. She is wearing cut-offs and a denim shirt and carrying a bag of groceries. She speaks quickly and choppily.

                              MARTHA
        Hi.

Jill sees Martha in the reflection before she turns around. She is surprised and glad to see her. That is, she's glad to see *somebody* she knows, even if it's only an acquaintance.

                               JILL
        Martha!

TWO SHOT - JILL AND MARTHA

Jill turns to face Martha.

                               JILL
                           (continuing)
        Well -- hi. How've you been?

                              MARTHA
        Oh, not too well . . . no, okay. How're you?

                               JILL
        Fine. Here for the weekend?

                              MARTHA
        No, I'm living here now.

                               JILL
        Oh. Then that's why I haven't seen you at softball practice.

                              MARTHA
        I've been here six months. Donna didn't tell you?

                               JILL
        No.

                              MARTHA
        Figures.

                               JILL
        I haven't seen Donna either . . . well, how do you like it here?

                              MARTHA
        It's all right.

                               JILL
        Pretty quiet in the winter, I guess.

                              MARTHA
        I don't mind that. I needed some quiet. That's why I left town. I couldn't take it. I mean, it was really an impossible situation.

                               JILL
        Oh.

MARTHA
(shifting her grocery bag)
I was seeing Celeste and Donna. And they were seeing each other.
That was bad enough, right?

JILL
(not thrilled to hear this whole story)
I guess so.

MARTHA
Then -- Linda comes back from San Francisco. You know Linda?
Celeste's old girlfriend? From college? No? Tufts?

Jill shakes her head. Martha keeps trying.

MARTHA
(describing Linda)
About my height? Short curly hair? Thirtyish? Therapist?

JILL
You're describing half the women I know.

MARTHA
(giving up)
Anyway, she came back, and I started seeing her, too.

JILL
And Celeste? *And* Donna?

MARTHA
And Celeste. And Donna. And Kate, only not for long because her
lover found out . . . but anyway, then -- Linda tells me *she's* seeing
Celeste and Donna.

JILL
(curious)
Together?

MARTHA
No. Well . . . maybe once. But anyway, that was it. I couldn't
handle it. Too many feelings. I had to back off. So I moved down
here.

JILL
That's good. Life's simpler here, huh?

MARTHA
(shifting her bag again)
Oh, I wish . . . but the woman I came down here with -- Fran?
Allen? Do you know her?

JILL
Um -- I don't think so.

MARTHA
Really? She knows *you.* Anyway, she's an old lover of Kate's, and
so am I, and so is Nancy.

                    JILL
                 (mystified)
Who's Nancy?

                   MARTHA
She's who we're living with. She's lovers with Annie . . . who's
another old lover of Linda's. So . . . guess who's coming down for
the weekend?

                    JILL
                 (guessing)
Linda.

                   MARTHA
No. Kate . . . who just broke up with Stephanie and wants to see
me. Only Fran doesn't know.

                    JILL
Does Nancy?

                   MARTHA
No! Nancy doesn't know either. God -- how do I get myself into
these things? Maybe I should move to New York.

                    JILL
Or the Gobi desert.

                   MARTHA
Is that in New Mexico?

                    JILL
No.

                   MARTHA
I can never go out there. You know Taos? That's where Lindsey
and Sheila are. And Belinda's in Albuquerque.

                    JILL
More old lovers?

                   MARTHA
                  (groans)
Please, don't remind me.
                (looking at her watch)
Oh, God -- I have to go. I should've been home two hours ago.
                (shifting her bag and touching Jill's arm)
Hey, it was good to see you.

                    JILL
You too.

Martha moves close to Jill's ear.

                   MARTHA
Listen, if you see Fran, don't say anything about what I've told you.

                              JILL
I won't.

                             MARTHA
Don't even mention that you saw me.

                              JILL
No, I won't.

                             MARTHA
Promise?

                              JILL
I don't know Fran.

                             MARTHA
Are you sure?
                        (describing Fran)
About my height? Short curly hair? Thirtyish? Therapist?

                              JILL
Nope.

                             MARTHA
She knows you . . . well, good seeing you. Come by sometime.
Martha hurries away.

MED. SHOT - JILL

She begins to stroll aimlessly down the sidewalk.

                           JILL (V.O.)
How could I "come by?" I don't know where she lives. I don't
think I *want* to know. God, what messes people make . . .
                            (beat)
I don't want to make a mess. Maybe I don't even want a commitment
. . . not even with the love of my life . . . if I can find her . . .
because that's how things *really* get complicated. Messy.
Jill watches a leather dyke ride by on her big motorcycle.

                              JILL
                          (continuing)
Maybe all I want is some good, clean, uncomplicated lust.

                                              DISSOLVE TO:

INT. THE BIKER'S GARAGE (JILL'S FANTASY) - NIGHT

Jill is in a garage where a huge motorcycle is parked. The place is lit by hanging
trouble lights, and all the corners are dark.

Jill is stripped to the waist, and her arms are tied to restraint cuffs on chains
hanging from the ceiling. Her legs are spread apart and her feet are bare and
also bound to the floor.

O.S. a WHIP CRACKS. Jill RATTLES her CHAINS.

36   Julia Willis

JILL
(speaking to someone O.S.; casually)
You know, this is something I always wanted to try.

Again the WHIP CRACKS, and Jill jumps nervously.

JILL
(continuing)
One of those things you never seem to get around to . . . like
skydiving. Or gourmet cooking.

CRACK.

JILL
(continuing)
Or making a will.

The BIKER comes INTO VIEW, the whip in her hand, dressed from head to toe in leather and chains. She is one mean mother. When she speaks, she mumbles monosyllables and sounds like Clint Eastwood's sister.

JILL
(continuing)
I'm sorry . . . I don't believe I caught your name.

CRACK.

BIKER
Spike.

JILL
Spike. That's a nice name.
(after a pause)
I had a hamster once named Spike.

CRACK.

JILL
(continuing)
The cat got him.

The Biker approaches Jill with the butt end of the whip in her hand. She is chewing gum. She spits it on the floor.

JILL
Juicy Fruit?

BIKER
No.

The Biker touches Jill's throat with the butt end of the whip.

JILL
(swallowing hard)
Uh -- did you see "Desert Hearts?"

BIKER
No.

Once Upon a Dream

She runs the butt down Jill's chest between her breasts and stops where her pants button.

JILL

What sort of movies *do* you like?

BIKER

Scary ones.

She pushes the butt lightly into Jill's stomach. Jill gasps, realizing that she has miscalculated -- this scene is not for her. She still tries to pretend they're simply dating and getting acquainted.

JILL

Do you smoke?

BIKER

Only when I'm set on fire.

Jill laughs uncertainly. The Biker walks around to Jill's back. This causes Jill to RATTLE her CHAINS nervously.

JILL

My -- my favorite food's Chinese. What's -- what's yours?

BIKER

Steak. Rare. Bloody.

The Biker rubs the butt end of the whip across Jill's ass and taps it lightly. Jill jumps.

JILL

Oh! You know, I hope this doesn't hurt too much, because I have an awfully low pain threshold.

BIKER

Good.

She taps Jill's ass harder.

JILL
(she *felt* that)
Ow! Maybe I should come back another time.

The Biker laughs cruelly.

JILL
(continuing)
When you're in a better mood.

The Biker smacks Jill's ass much harder this time.

JILL
(continuing)
OW! Okay, fun's fun -- I have to go now. I think I left the cake running and a water in the oven.

The Biker CRACKS her whip. Jill RATTLES her CHAINS.

                              JILL
                          (continuing)
           Oh, there goes the doorbell! Coming!

                                                         CUT TO:

INT. A LEATHER SHOP - DAY

Jill stands transfixed by a table of leather goods with studs on them, her
back to the shop window. She is holding a riding crop in her hand.

In the b.g. on the street we SEE the Dreamgirl pass by the window. Jill
comes back to reality and shudders.

                              JILL
                           (relieved)
    Whew.

A young SHOPGIRL comes over to Jill.

                            SHOPGIRL
                          (innocently)
    May I help you?

Jill jumps back from the table.

                              JILL
    No, no – I'm just looking.

She discovers the riding crop in her hand and drops it like a hot potato.

                              JILL
                          (continuing)
    Oh, no, I'm not looking, I'm – I'm not interested.

Jill hurries out of the shop. The Shopgirl exchanges a look with another
customer and shrugs.

EXT. AN OUTDOOR CAFE ON COMMERCIAL STREET

Jill is sitting alone, having a cappuccino, no closer than ever to finding love,
lust, or her Dreamgirl.

                            JILL (V.O.)
    No. If I were a real masochist, I'd be passing for straight.

Her table is right by the sidewalk. She watches a STRAIGHT COUPLE walking
past the cafe. The man (who's taller) has his arm around the woman's
shoulders, so the woman is walking very awkwardly. Jill shakes her head
sadly, and the couple keeps going.

From the other direction TWO WOMEN go by, holding hands, and neither
has trouble walking. Jill smiles. As they pass the cafe, Jill overhears a
STRAIGHT WOMAN at a table behind her.

STRAIGHT WOMAN
Oh no – look at that! We should've stayed in Hyannis.

Jill turns to look at the Straight Woman. She is sunburned, wearing a sundress and dark, tacky sunglasses. Sitting with her is HER FRIEND, another woman, in shorts. They both wear too much jewelry, like earrings and matching necklaces shaped like gilded potato chips.

Both women are probably from the same secretarial pool and are drinking pink Cape Codders in tall glasses with little parasols.

STRAIGHT WOMAN
I mean, I don't care what they do in private, but to go around like that in public – yuck.

Her Friend gives an embarrassed smile. The Straight Woman is talking too loud, while finishing her third Cape Codder.

STRAIGHT WOMAN
(continuing)
It's not something I want to *see*. I mean, it's advertising the fact. They might as well be out on the streets recruiting people – normal people, like you and me.

HER FRIEND
(self-conscious)
Claire, please – not so loud.

A WAITER approaches their table with fresh Cape Codders. He is obviously a faggot.

STRAIGHT WOMAN
Oh, why the hell not?

WAITER
(stage whisper)
Because they might hear you.

STRAIGHT WOMAN
Oh, piss on them!

The Waiter has served Her Friend. He picks up the other drink on his tray and pours it in the Straight Woman's lap.

WAITER
Piss on you, sweetheart.

He tears up their tab and walks away. People at the surrounding tables applaud. The Straight Woman sputters and fumes and storms off. Her Friend leaves a tip and goes after her.

Jill has been watching this scene with some amusement. Now she returns to her cappuccino and her thoughts.

DISSOLVE TO:

Julia Willis

EXT. A CARD TABLE OUTSIDE TOWN HALL (JILL'S FANTASY) - DAY - TIGHT ANGLE - POSTER

We are LOOKING at a poster of Jill dressed as Uncle Sam (but without the beard) saying "I WANT YOU!" CAMERA PULLS BACK TO REVEAL Jill, sitting at a table beside the poster with a clipboard and a stack of papers, looking very official. She's dressed as Uncle Sam and is processing a line of a dozen women and one old hippie.

Her ASSISTANT is going down the line handing out applications and pencils, saying AD LIBS like "Fill this out, please" and "Keep the line moving, please."

                          JILL
     Next!

A YOUNG COLLEGE GIRL hands in her application. Jill looks it over.

                          JILL
                       (continuing)
     All right, Mary. And why would you like to be a lesbian?

                    YOUNG COLLEGE GIRL
                       (guessing)
     The Spanish class was full?

Jill rips up her application.

                          JILL
     Nope – sorry. Next!

The Young College Girl walks away, head down, and a JOCK takes her place. Jill reads from her application.

                          JILL
                       (continuing)
     Chris.
                       (beat)
     I see you played basketball in high school *and* college.

                          JOCK
                       (proudly)
     And my gym teacher let me wear her whistle.

                          JILL
     Good, good.
                       (pointing)
     Have a seat over there and we'll call you.

                          JOCK
     All right!

The Jock gives Jill five and goes happily off, waving her fists in the air. A VERY POLITICALLY CORRECT WOMAN comes up. She is deadly serious.

                          JILL
                       (reading)
     Okay ... Emily.

Once Upon a Dream   41

>   V.P. CORRECT WOMAN
>   (blurting it out)
> It's extremely important that I be disowned by my reactionary family
> as soon as possible!

>   JILL
> Well, I'm sure that can be arranged. Go sit over there and see if
> you can lighten up a little.

The Very Politically Correct Woman marches off, and an OLD HIPPIE (a guy
with long hair, a headband, and a peace symbol around his neck) steps up.

>   JILL
> Yes?

>   OLD HIPPIE
> Is this the line for the Dead tickets?

>   JILL
> No, man -- sorry.

>   OLD HIPPIE
> Oh, wow. Bummer.

He wanders off, shaking his head. Jill gives him a peace sign.

>   JILL
> Far out.

When she turns back to the line, the Dreamgirl is in front of her. The Dreamgirl
holds out her application and Jill reaches for it.

>   JILL
> Hi.

>   DREAMGIRL
> Hello.

They are both holding onto the application and looking into one another's
eyes.

>   JILL
> Would you like to sign up?

>   DREAMGIRL
> I already did. Ages ago.

>   JILL
> Wonderful.

                                                        CUT TO:

EXT. A CARD TABLE OUTSIDE TOWN HALL - DAY

Jill finds herself in front of a card table, signing a petition against the dumping
of nuclear waste. A poster next to the table says "STOP NUCLEAR WASTE!"

The Very Politically Correct Woman from Jill's fantasy is talking to her and
showing her an ugly color picture of a blob.

Julia Willis

V.P. CORRECT WOMAN
Now it's too late! Mutant sponges like this one are roaming the Bay. They range from ten to fifty feet in length, and they're feeding on sharks, windsurfers, and small pleasure craft.

JILL
Gee, I hope they run into Norman Mailer.

Jill walks away as the Very Politically Correct Woman continues shouting.

V.P. CORRECT WOMAN
This is no joke, people! We need your help to stop these sponges!

Jill is heading back toward the guesthouse.

JILL (V.O.)
(puzzling over it)
If I were a Dreamgirl, where would I be? . . . I wonder if Leslie would let me borrow her car?

EXT. THE BEACH AT RACE POINT - FULL SHOT - THE DREAMGIRL

The Dreamgirl has driven out to Race Point. Her car is parked in the lot by the dunes. She is leaning against the hood, looking up and down the beach. She seems to be waiting for someone.

EXT. THE GUESTHOUSE - OUTSIDE ROOM NUMBER SEVEN

Jill finds a "DO NOT DISTURB" sign on the door. She starts to knock but changes her mind and goes to sit on a bench between number seven and number eight. She listens for sounds coming from number seven.

JILL (V.O.)
I don't hear anything. Maybe they're asleep. It's been two hours. They can't still be at it, can they? After being together so long? I mean – six years . . .

Two JOGGING WOMEN in matching outfits run up to the door of number eight. One of the women opens the door with a key while the other one runs in place. Then they go into number eight together, breathing heavily from the exercise, and close the door.

JILL (V.O.)
I should start exercising more. I'll bet those two have an incredible sex life. Two bodies working together like a well-oiled machine . . .

DISSOLVE TO:

INT. BATHROOM/ROOM NUMBER EIGHT (JILL'S FANTASY) - DAY

The two Jogging Women are in the bathroom, pulling off their running outfits to shower. The SHOWER is RUNNING. Their bodies are shiny with sweat and nicely muscled.

(CONTINUED)

CONTINUED:

One steps into the shower, followed by the other. They wash one another's bodies, but the washing soon turns into lovemaking. The sex is very hot and energetic. One comes standing up in the shower while the other goes down on her.

Then they come out of the shower (leaving it running) and, with their bodies still wet, they lie down on the tiles amid a pile of fluffy towels, and one brings the other to orgasm with her hand.

The towels are white, the tiles are black, their bodies glisten, and the SOUND OF THE SHOWER is steady and constant. Only their muffled cries of passion rise above it.

OVERHEAD SHOT (JILL'S FANTASY) - THE TWO JOGGING WOMEN

We LOOK DOWN on their bodies, intertwined and at rest.

CUT TO:

EXT. OUTSIDE ROOM NUMBER SEVEN - DAY

Jill is practically panting. She talks to herself out loud.

JILL
I'm definitely joining a health club next week.

The Jogging Women come out of room number eight. They are still fully dressed in their running attire, and they are bickering. They don't even acknowledge Jill's presence.

ONE JOGGING WOMAN
I always change my Tampax *before* I run.

OTHER JOGGING WOMAN
So do I. I just forgot, okay?

ONE JOGGING WOMAN
Now we won't have time to go all the way to Race Point.

OTHER JOGGING WOMAN
Then fuck Race Point!

She slams the door to their room.

ONE JOGGING WOMAN
Have you got the key?

OTHER JOGGING WOMAN
What?

ONE JOGGING WOMAN
The key — the key — the key to the room.

The Other Jogging Woman realizes she's locked the door with the key inside.

                    OTHER JOGGING WOMAN
It's on the dresser.

                    ONE JOGGING WOMAN
                    (throwing up her hands)
I don't believe it!

                    OTHER JOGGING WOMAN
                    (defensive)
The manager can let us in.

The Other Jogging Woman starts to run.

                    ONE JOGGING WOMAN
First the Tampax, now this!

She follows the Other Jogging Woman off.

                    OTHER JOGGING WOMAN (O.S.)
Just shut up, will you?

                    ONE JOGGING WOMAN (O.S.)
Is this how the whole weekend is going to be?

                    OTHER JOGGING WOMAN (O.S.)
Yes! Satisfied? Yes!

They're gone. Jill has been watching them with a mixture of horror and fascination. Again she speaks to herself aloud.

                    JILL
Damn, girl – that's some vivid imagination you got there.

She takes another look at the "DO NOT DISTURB" sign on the door of number seven and puts her chin in her hand to wait.

EXT. THE BEACH AT RACE POINT - LATE AFTERNOON

The Dreamgirl looks at her watch, sighs, and gets back in her car. She's given up waiting.

EXT. OUTSIDE ROOM NUMBER SEVEN - LATE AFTERNOON - CLOSEUP - "DO NOT DISTURB" SIGN

The sign is still hanging on the door.

ANGLE ON JILL

She is still sitting on the bench, waiting. Just like the Dreamgirl, she looks at her watch and sighs.

OUTSIDE ROOM NUMBER SEVEN - FULL SHOT

The door opens and Laura and Leslie come out. They are dressed casually but nicely for dinner.

LAURA
(surprised)
Jill — what are you doing out here?

JILL
(indicating the sign)
I'm "not disturbing" you.

Leslie takes the "DO NOT DISTURB" sign off the doorknob.

LESLIE
(embarrassed)
Oops.

LAURA
(puzzled)
How did *that* get there?

LESLIE
I put it there.

LAURA
When?

LESLIE
Ages ago. When you were in the bathroom.

LAURA
(to Jill)
And how long have you been sitting out here?

JILL
I don't know. Have I grown?
(standing up)
Do I look taller?

LESLIE
Oh, Jill — I'm sorry. I just wanted us to have a little privacy after
— and I forgot.

LAURA
Poor Jill.

JILL
Oh, that's all right.

LAURA
(to Jill)
You're not having fun yet.

LESLIE
(to Laura)
Well, don't *tell* her, *ask* her.
(to Jill)
Did you find your Dreamgirl?

                    LAURA
You can see she didn't.

                    JILL
              (a little defensive)
Not yet ... but I know I will.

                    LESLIE
Atta girl. Think positive.

She starts to close the door to their room.

                    JILL
              (thinking of the Jogging Women)
Wait! Got the key?

Leslie pats her pocket and closes the door.

                    LESLIE
Sure.

                    JILL
Oh.

                    LAURA
We're going to the Lobster Pot. Come with us.

                    JILL
This early?

                    LESLIE
Before it gets crowded.

                    LAURA
Then we're going out on the beach to watch the sunset ... come on.

                    JILL
No — you've got a romantic evening all planned.

                    LESLIE
All right, you can skip the beach part ... but come to dinner.

                    LAURA
Please.

                    JILL
              (indecisive)
Oh, I don't know.

                    LAURA
You've got to eat.

                    JILL
Yeah ...

                    LESLIE
Maybe your Dreamgirl'll be at the Lobster Pot.

                         LAURA
That's right.

                          JILL
                      (interested)
Yeah -- she could be, couldn't she?

                         LESLIE
Sure she could. Best lobsters in town.

                         LAURA
Sure. Come on.

                          JILL
Okay.

They start to walk down the street, but Laura stops.

                         LAURA
Oh, wait -- let's go the other way. I know a short cut.

                         LESLIE
You must be hungry.

                         LAURA
                (turning to go the other way)
I'm famished. Must be the salt air.

                         LESLIE
Or the company?

Leslie playfully bites Laura's shoulder. Laura screams.

                          JILL
                        (campy)
Girls, please!

EXT. A SIDE STREET OFF COMMERCIAL STREET

Laura, Leslie, and Jill are walking up the side street. It's Laura's short cut,
so she's leading the way. Jill is regaling them with the story of the Waiter
in the outdoor cafe.

                          JILL
-- and then he poured the Cape Codder right in her lap.

                         LESLIE
Fantastic!

                         LAURA
                (touching her crotch)
Ooh -- that must've been cold.

                          JILL
She wouldn't have noticed. I'm sure she's permanently frozen below
the waist by now.

Laura stops short. She is looking ahead of them.

> **LAURA**
> (pointing)
>
> **Oh, look – isn't that – ?**

Leslie stops, too.

> **LESLIE**
>
> **It sure is.**

Jill is bringing up the rear, looking behind them, walking backwards. She bumps into Leslie.

> **LAURA**
>
> **Jill, look!**

They all look. The Dreamgirl's car is parked just up the street near the corner of Commercial Street.

> **JILL**
> (jumping for joy)
>
> **There she is, there she is!**

EXT. THE DREAMGIRL'S PARKED CAR

Jill rushes over to the car, with Laura and Leslie sauntering along behind her. She puts her hands on the car to make sure it's real. It is. The top is up now, and the doors are locked.

> **JILL**
> (so pleased)
>
> **Now we're getting somewhere.**

Laura and Leslie arrive at the car. Laura looks inside, expecting to see the Dreamgirl.

> **LAURA**
>
> **Where'd she go?**

> **LESLIE**
> (explaining; to Laura)
>
> **I think it's just the car.**

> **LAURA**
> (to Jill)
>
> **Oh – didn't you see her?**

> **JILL**
>
> **Uh – no, but now we know she's here. Somewhere.**

Jill pats the car.

> **LESLIE**
>
> **Yeah, anywhere.**

> **LAURA**
>
> **At least she's not in Truro.**

JILL

Exactly — she's here. And I know the car hasn't been here long.

LAURA

How?

JILL

Because I would've seen it this afternoon, from Commercial Street. I know I would've ... and besides —

Jill goes to the front of the car and puts her hands on the hood.

JILL
(continuing; proudly)

— it's still warm.

LESLIE
(British accent)

Ah — excellent, Watson.

Jill keeps her hands on the hood, communing with the Dreamgirl's spirit.

JILL

She's close by — I can feel it.

LAURA

See? She's probably at the Lobster Pot. Let's go find her.

Laura takes Leslie's arm to lead her on.

LESLIE
(to Jill)

Come along, dear. The game's afoot.

Jill is planted in front of the car.

JILL

Maybe I better stay here ... for when she comes back.

LAURA

But she could be hours ...

Jill points to the parking meter.

JILL

No — she only has twenty minutes left on the meter.

LESLIE

You think of everything.

JILL

I'll wait here, and when she comes back I'll ask her to dinner.

LAURA

Oh, Jill ...

JILL

Go ahead. Have a great lobster. I'll be fine.

Julia Willis

LESLIE

Good luck.

LAURA
(reluctant)

Okay – see you later then.

Laura and Leslie go on toward the Lobster Pot.

JILL

Bye.

She beams at the car and looks around expectantly, sure that her Dreamgirl will appear any second.

JILL (V.O.)
(planning their evening)

Yeah, dinner. A long, slow, sexy dinner ... lobsters and melted butter ... hope she's not a vegetarian ...

DISSOLVE TO:

INT. TABLE FOR TWO IN A RESTAURANT (JILL'S FANTASY) - EVENING

Jill and the Dreamgirl are eating dinner. They devour their lobsters, dipping chunks of meat in the butter and looking hungrily into one another's eyes. They never say a word and don't have to -- their thoughts are very clear.

CLOSEUPS of eyes and lips and fingers (a parody of the famous dinner scene from "TOM JONES").

EXT. THE BEACH AT RACE POINT (JILL'S FANTASY) - MOONLIGHT

Jill and the Dreamgirl are lying on the beach, on an oval mattress fashioned in the shape of a purplish-pink vulva.

They are both naked and draped in its liplike folds. They sip champagne in long-stemmed glasses and make slow, sensuous love.

EXT. ANY BEACH (JILL'S FANTASY) - DAY FOR NIGHT - (STOCK)

STOCK FOOTAGE (preferably in black and white) of waves crashing on the shore.

JILL (V.O.)

No, maybe not ... maybe after all that greasy lobster we should have a shower.

INT. BATHROOM/ROOM NUMBER EIGHT (JILL'S FANTASY)

Jill and the Dreamgirl are standing naked in a shower. This is the same shower the Jogging Women used earlier. They are kissing passionately, but the water isn't running.

The shower door is opened by one of the Jogging Women. Jill and the Dreamgirl continue kissing, as One Jogging Woman speaks to the other in a snippy tone.

ONE JOGGING WOMAN
What are *they* doing in *our* shower?

OTHER JOGGING WOMAN
How the hell should I know?

CUT TO:

EXT. A SIDE STREET OFF COMMERCIAL STREET - DUSK - CLOSEUP - PARKING METER

That twenty minutes on the meter has long since run out, and the red violation flag is up.

THE DREAMGIRL'S PARKED CAR

The sun is setting, and Jill is still standing by the Dreamgirl's car. She is getting very hungry. Someone walks by eating a slice of pizza, and Jill's eyes follow her, concentrating on the pizza.

A BABYDYKE who has been watching Jill with interest finally makes her move.

BABYDYKE
(coming over; pointing to the car)
Having trouble?

JILL
Huh?

BABYDYKE
Want me to take a look at it?

JILL
Oh -- thanks, but there's nothing wrong with the car.

BABYDYKE
Oh.
(beat; referring to the car)
It's wicked nice.

JILL
It's not mine.

Jill tries to be friendly without giving the Babydyke too much encouragement. This is not so simple, because the Babydyke is not easily discouraged.

BABYDYKE
Oh ... are you waiting for someone?

JILL
Uh -- yeah. Sort of.

BABYDYKE
I think they've stood you up.

JILL
Why do you say that?

BABYDYKE

No offense. I just see you waiting around for like an hour, and that's -- you know.

The Babydyke shrugs and holds out her hand. Jill looks at it hesitantly.

BABYDYKE

My name's Kristie.

Jill shakes her hand. The Babydyke holds on to it.

JILL

Jill.

BABYDYKE

Nice to meet you . . . um -- do you dance?

Jill smiles tolerantly as she takes her hand back.

JILL

Occasionally.

BABYDYKE

Um -- have you been to the Pied Piper?

JILL

Not today.

BABYDYKE

I bet you're a good dancer.

JILL

Oh, I don't know . . .

BABYDYKE

I bet you are. Um -- you wanta come?
(beat; flustered)
To the Pied, I mean.

JILL

Not right now, thanks.

Jill looks up and down the street, still watching out for the Dreamgirl but also seeking an escape route. The Babydyke persists.

BABYDYKE

I don't think she's coming.

JILL
(changing the subject)
How old are you?

BABYDYKE
(quickly)
Twenty-three.

She shuffles her feet nervously. She's obviously lying.

Once Upon a Dream   53

JILL
(doubting her)
I don't think so.

BABYDYKE
(insistent)
I been around. It's not my first time.

JILL
That's good to know.

BABYDYKE
Yeah, you'll like me once you get to know me.

Jill thinks of a way to put the Babydyke to good use and get rid of her for a while.

JILL
(very direct)
Listen -- would you like to do me a favor?

The Babydyke thinks Jill is angry. She takes a step backward.

BABYDYKE
Don't get mad.

JILL
No, I'm serious.

BABYDYKE
(eager)
Sure ... anything.

JILL
Let's not get carried away.

Jill takes out her wallet and removes a five-dollar bill.

BABYDYKE
(seeing the money)
I know where there's some grass.

JILL
No, no – I'm cool. Have you eaten?

BABYDYKE
Uh – yeah. But I could watch you.

JILL
You know that takeout place around the corner?

BABYDYKE
You mean Mojo's?

Jill offers the Babydyke the five-dollar bill.

                            JILL
Yeah. Take this, and get me a couple of slices of pizza. And get
yourself one, too, if you want it.

                          BABYDYKE
                      (refusing her money)
Oh, no -- this is on me. I'll be right back.

The Babydyke dashes off. Jill wonders if she's giving the Babydyke too much
hope.

                            JILL
                        (to herself)
Was that a mistake?

The Babydyke rushes back and slams into Jill. Their faces are almost touching.

                          BABYDYKE
                      (out of breath)
Oh, Jill -- I forgot. What would you like to drink?

                            JILL
Nothing.

                          BABYDYKE
Sure?

                            JILL
Yes.

                          BABYDYKE
Okay -- I'll be right back.

She rushes off again.

                            JILL
                  (calling to the Babydyke)
Don't fall!
                        (to herself)
Definitely a mistake.

EXT. THE BEACH BY COMMERCIAL STREET - NIGHT

Laura and Leslie have had a wonderful lobster dinner and a beautiful sunset.
They are strolling along the beach, holding hands.

                           LAURA
This is so perfect.

                           LESLIE
God, I'm stuffed.

They stop. Leslie burps politely.

                           LAURA
Now *that's* not very romantic, dear.

Once Upon a Dream   55

                    LESLIE
I'm sorry -- how about this?
                    (hand over her heart)
Darling, my heart is full.

                    LAURA
That's better.

They kiss and walk another step or two.

                    LESLIE
                    (teasing)
And so's my stomach -- much *too* full -- oof.

Laura slaps at Leslie playfully.

                    LAURA
Oh, stop! Are you glad we came?

                    LESLIE
                    (reacting to the slap)
Ow! Okay, okay -- no hits below the belly.

                    LAURA
You and your belly. Are you glad we came or not?

                    LESLIE
I am very, very, *very* glad ... and you know it or you wouldn't
have asked me.

                    LAURA
                    (laughing)
I love coming back here with you.

                    LESLIE
                    (holding her stomach)
Wonder where I could get an Alka-Seltzer?

Laura raises her hand again, and Leslie grabs it.

                    LESLIE
Kidding, just kidding.

                    LAURA
Uh-huh.
                    (beat)
And is it all right we brought Jill?

                    LESLIE
Sure. I don't mind Jill. She's just a little --

                    LAURA
-- obsessive?

                    LESLIE
She's just been alone too long.

Julia Willis

EXT. A SIDE STREET OFF COMMERCIAL STREET - NIGHT - THE DREAMGIRL'S PARKED CAR

Jill is waiting for the Babydyke with her pizza. The two Jogging Women from the guesthouse pass by, bickering again.

> ONE JOGGING WOMAN
> If you don't like it, why did you order it?

> OTHER JOGGING WOMAN
> I didn't know that's what it was.

> ONE JOGGING WOMAN
> How could you not know? It said very plainly on the menu -- "stuffed."

> OTHER JOGGING WOMAN
> Okay, okay.

They go out of sight, but not out of hearing.

> ONE JOGGING WOMAN (O.S.)
> What does "stuffed" mean to you?

> OTHER JOGGING WOMAN (O.S.)
> I don't know, never mind, just forget it. Jesus Christ!

Jill leans on the hood and sighs.

EXT. THE TAKE-OUT LINE AT MOJO'S

The Babydyke tries to balance the pizza on a paper plate with one hand while putting away her wallet with the other. A huge cup of soda is sitting on the counter beside the straws and napkins.

When she gets her wallet into her back pocket (where else?), she picks up the cup with her free hand and then realizes she can't reach for the napkins. She needs an extra hand.

> BABYDYKE
> Oh, shit.

Suddenly, the Dreamgirl appears at her side, getting her some napkins and a straw. She tucks the napkins under the pizza plate and puts the straw in the cup.

> BABYDYKE
> (to the Dreamgirl)
> Hey, thanks a lot.

The Dreamgirl just smiles and moves away. The Babydyke turns and scurries back to Jill.

EXT. A SIDE STREET OFF COMMERCIAL STREET - THE CORNER

Laura and Leslie, on their way to the Pied Piper to dance, stop on the corner and see Jill just where they left her hours before.

Once Upon a Dream

LESLIE

Oh no ...

LAURA
(her voice full of pity)

Jill.

LESLIE

Now I *do* need an Alka-Seltzer.

THE DREAMGIRL'S PARKED CAR

They join Jill, who is a little embarrassed to see them. She stops leaning
on the car.

JILL

Hi. Back already?

LESLIE

Why don't you just break the windshield and move right on in?

JILL

Ha-ha.

LAURA
(overly sympathetic)

Oh, she hasn't come back ... and you're still waiting.

JILL

Yeah, well, don't make it sound like somebody's died.

LAURA

Have you had any dinner?

JILL
(lying)

Sure, I had dinner.

LAURA

What? What did you have?

JILL
(irritable)

I picked something up, okay?

LESLIE
(to Laura)

Easy, little mother.

LAURA
(to Jill)

Well, good.
(beat)

We had a great dinner.

JILL

Good.

LAURA

We're going to the Pied now.

JILL
(stubborn)

Uh-huh.

LESLIE

Maybe *that's* where she is.

LAURA

Yeah, the Pied. That's where I'd go . . .
(to Leslie)
. . . wouldn't you?

JILL

Well, if you see her --

The Babydyke rushes into the scene with her hands full of pizza and soda.

BABYDYKE
(explaining; to Jill)

There was a big line.

She sees Laura and Leslie looking at her and at Jill and becomes even more self-conscious.

BABYDYKE
(to Laura and Leslie)

Hi.

LAURA/LESLIE
(together)

Hello.

Jill has been caught in her lie about dinner and with a babydyke on her hands as well.

JILL

Uh -- this is Kristen.

BABYDYKE

Kristie.

JILL

Right.
(reaching)
Here, let me take that.

Jill puts the pizza on the hood of the Dreamgirl's car and holds the huge cup of soda awkwardly in both hands.

BABYDYKE

I hope you like Pepsi.

JILL

Yeah -- sure -- fine.

BABYDYKE
I knew you'd be thirsty.

Laura and Leslie exchange a look. Jill would very much like to get rid of them.

JILL
(to Laura and Leslie)
Okay -- well, go ahead, and maybe I'll catch up with you later.

LESLIE
(teasing)
You're way ahead of me already.

Laura elbows Leslie in the side.

LAURA
(to Jill)
Maybe we'll see you there, then.

JILL
Yeah, maybe so.

LESLIE
(still teasing)
Don't do anyone I wouldn't do.

JILL
(sarcastic)
Thanks a lot.

LAURA
(friendly)
Bye, Kristie.

Laura and Leslie walk off, grinning broadly. The Babydyke calls after them.

BABYDYKE
Nice to meet you!
(to Jill)
Friends of yours?

JILL
(eating her pizza)
Yeah -- I'm sorry -- I didn't introduce everybody.

BABYDYKE
That's okay. Eat. Enjoy. Mangia.
(beat)
I *knew* you'd like Pepsi. It's my favorite, too.

With her mouth full of pizza, Jill rolls her eyes.

Julia Willis

INT. BAR - THE PIED PIPER

In the bar women are dancing and milling about.

ANGLE ON DJ

The DJ in the booth makes her opening remarks.

> **DJ**
> Good evening, ladies and funky women, and welcome to the Pied.
> My name is Rickie, and I'll be your attendant on this all-disco night
> flight. So get down and boogie ...

She turns up the MUSIC ("I LOVE THE NIGHTLIFE"/Alicia Bridges).

SLOW PAN TO DJ'S RIGHT

Near the DJ booth the Dreamgirl is sitting at the bar alone. She has her
back to the bartender and her elbows resting on the bar. There is a drink
in her hand, but she's barely touched it.

She is looking out over the room and the dancers as if she's searching for
someone. A woman asks her to dance, but she declines politely.

EXT. IN THE WELL-LIT ALLEY OUTSIDE THE PIED PIPER

"I LOVE THE NIGHTLIFE" is still PLAYING inside. There is a sign above
the door to the bar that reads "TONIGHT ONLY - DISCOMANIA."

A woman at the door, the DOORPERSON, is checking I.D.s and taking in
a small cover charge. Laura and Leslie come up to the door just as someone
they know, POLLY, is on her way out.

> **LAURA**
> Polly – hi!

Polly has been speaking to the Doorperson, and now she turns to Laura and
Leslie. AD LIB hellos all around.

> **LAURA**
> Leaving so soon?

> **LESLIE**
> (imitating the Wicked Witch of the West)
> Why, we won't hear of it!

> **LAURA**
> Come sit with us.

> **POLLY**
> No, I gotta go down to the Pilgrim House and catch a band. I might
> want to book them in town.
> (to the Doorperson)
> Besides, disco *still* sucks.

Once Upon a Dream   61

The Doorperson gives Polly a "So what?" look.

LAURA
Oh, goody. It's nostalgia night.

LESLIE
(Bette Davis)
She adores cheap sentiment.

POLLY
Yeah, well, she can have it.

Leslie hands the Doorperson two dollars.

LESLIE
Want to see our I.D.s?

DOORPERSON
That's okay.

LESLIE
(to Laura)
That's funny – I always used to get carded in disco bars.

LAURA
We must be getting old.

LESLIE
Speak for yourself.

They AD LIB good-byes to Polly and go inside. Now Polly confronts the Doorperson.

POLLY
So – do I get my dollar back?

DOORPERSON
You want your dollar back?

POLLY
I was only in there five minutes.

The Doorperson gives her a dollar.

DOORPERSON
Take the damn thing, I don't care.

POLLY
Thanks.

As Polly leaves, the Doorperson makes a comment to herself:

DOORPERSON
Why are dykes so fucking cheap?

EXT. THE DREAMGIRL'S PARKED CAR

Jill has finished her pizza. She is trying to read a local free paper by streetlight. Her empty plate and napkin are on the hood of the Dreamgirl's car.

The Babydyke holds the huge cup of Pepsi in both hands and, with the straw in her mouth, slurps the bottom. This makes a terrible NOISE, and Jill winces.

                    BABYDYKE
    Aah! All gone. Want some dessert?

                      JILL
                (reading the paper)
    No thanks.

The Babydyke picks up the plate and napkin and sees a trash barrel just across the street.

                    BABYDYKE
    Be right back.

The Babydyke runs to the trash barrel while Jill pretends to read the paper and talks to herself.

                    JILL (V.O.)
    Where did I go wrong? Where's my Dreamgirl? I mean, am I asking
    for too much? Should I settle for a fling with a younger woman?

Jill watches the Babydyke playing with the trash, balling it up and shooting it like a basketball into the barrel. She misses and tries again.

                    JILL (V.O.)
                   (continuing)
    A *much* younger woman? . . .

                                              DISSOLVE TO:

EXT. A PORCH SWING IN JILL'S PAST (JILL'S FANTASY) - DAY

Jill and the Babydyke are swinging on the porch swing. They are both dressed in children's clothes.

Jill is wearing a Minnie Mouse T-shirt, jeans, and sneakers, and the Babydyke has on a short, frilly dress with patent leather shoes. Jill's hair is in two little ponytails. As in reality, the Babydyke is the initial aggressor.

                    BABYDYKE
    What do you want to do now?

                      JILL
    I don't know.

                    BABYDYKE
    Wanta play Barbie?

                      JILL
    Nah.

                              BABYDYKE
Wanta play cowgirl?

                                JILL
Nah.

                              BABYDYKE
I know – let's play doctor. I'll be the doctor and you be the nurse.

The Babydyke starts climbing on top of Jill.

                                JILL
                         (changing her mind)
Awright, let's play Barbie.

                              BABYDYKE
Okay, Nurse -- you got to take off your clothes so's I can examine
you.

                                JILL
                            (frowning)
That sounds like sexual harassment to me.

                              BABYDYKE
Nuh-uh – I'm the doctor and you got to do what I say.

The Babydyke rips Jill's T-shirt down the front (it tears easily) and exposes
her breasts. Jill is quickly aroused.

                                JILL
Ooh – I'm gonna tell.

She grabs the Babydyke and kisses her. The Babydyke panics and jumps up.

                              BABYDYKE
No, *I'm* gonna tell! Mama!

The Babydyke runs off, leaving Jill lying on the swing with her legs spread
and her breasts exposed.

                                JILL
                            (softly)
Ma-ma.

                                                            CUT TO:

EXT. THE DREAMGIRL'S PARKED CAR - NIGHT

Jill is still lost in her fantasy. The Babydyke returns from tossing paper wads
at the trash barrel.

                                JILL
                         (repeating herself)
Ma-ma.

                              BABYDYKE
Hey – Jill!

                    JILL
                (coming around)
Huh?

                    BABYDYKE
I said you missed my best shot.

                    JILL
Oh.
                (beat)
How old are you, really ... eighteen?

                    BABYDYKE
I told you — twenty-one. I look young for my age.

                    JILL
I thought you said twenty-three.

                    BABYDYKE
                (caught)
Right — twenty-three. What did I just say?

                    JILL
Twenty-one.

                    BABYDYKE
Oh. I — I meant twenty-three, I'm twenty-three.

Now Jill definitely doesn't believe her.

                    JILL
Uh-huh.

                    BABYDYKE
Want to see my I.D.?

                    JILL
That's okay.
                (back to her newspaper)
It's disco night at the Pied Piper. Remember disco?

                    BABYDYKE
Sure I do ... it sucked, right?

                    JILL
Oh, I don't know ... it had its moments.
                (beat)
I feel like I'm giving a history lesson.

                    BABYDYKE
Well, let's go to the Pied and do some disco.

                    JILL
Not just now.

Jill puts down the paper, looking bored. The Babydyke doesn't give up easily.

Once Upon a Dream

BABYDYKE
Want to go to a movie?

JILL
No.

BABYDYKE
Um – did you see "Desert Hearts?"

JILL
Uh-huh.

BABYDYKE
I saw it thirty-seven times. What was your favorite part?

JILL
The sex.

BABYDYKE
Mine, too ... from where she's in the motel room and she's just got that robe on, and Kay comes to the door ... wow.
(beat)
Where are you staying?

JILL
In a guesthouse.

BABYDYKE
I've got my own room at the Holiday Inn.

JILL
Good.

BABYDYKE
We could go over there and watch TV ... or do ... whatever we – uh – wanted to.

Jill has had enough. It's time to break the bad news.

JILL
Look – Kristen –

BABYDYKE
It's Kristie.

JILL
Kristie. This – this just isn't working. Now, you're very nice, but you're too young for me.

BABYDYKE
But I'm *not* –

JILL
Or I'm too old for *you* ... or something.
(beat)
Look, I have to say "no" here. "No, never, absolutely not." I would say "let's be friends," but I have a feeling that's not what you're looking for.

                         BABYDYKE
                         (pouting)
I got lots of friends.

                            JILL
I'm sure you do . . . and I wish you lots of lovers to go along with
them. Meanwhile, thanks for all your help, and — so long.

Jill waves, hoping the Babydyke will finally take the hint. She does, but she
doesn't take it too well.

                         BABYDYKE
That's just great — that's super. You could've told me that an hour
ago.

                            JILL
I'm sorry, I tried —

                         BABYDYKE
Oh, sure . . . well, I'm sorry, too. And you can bet I won't bother
you anymore.

The Babydyke takes two steps, then turns around and comes back. She
gets right up in Jill's face.

                         BABYDYKE
                         (continuing)
Because you know what you are? You're nothing but a C.T. — a
big, fat C.T.!

Jill watches as the Babydyke takes two more steps, then turns back and shouts.

                         BABYDYKE
                         (continuing)
AND THAT SPELLS CLIT-TEASE!

She marches off in the direction of Commercial Street. Several women passing
by look at Jill curiously. She smiles weakly and waves at them.

                            JILL
                    (to women passing)
Nice night.

INT. THE PIED PIPER - MED. SHOT - LAURA AND LESLIE

Laura and Leslie are sitting at a table, having a drink and laughing as the
MUSIC ("MORE, MORE, MORE"/The Andrea True Connection) PLAYS and
lots of women dance beside them. One woman practically has her ass on
their table.

They hold onto their drinks and laugh harder. Laura sings along with the
record.

EXT. THE DECK OUTSIDE THE PIED PIPER - CLOSE SHOT - THE DREAMGIRL

"MORE, MORE, MORE" CONTINUES. The Dreamgirl is on the deck, alone, still nursing the same drink she had inside.

She stands at the railing and looks first into the bar at the women dancing and then out to sea. Picking up her drink which was resting on the railing, she slowly pours it over the side into the sand.

EXT. A SIDE STREET OFF COMMERCIAL STREET

Jill is leaning dejectedly against the trash barrel across from the Dreamgirl's car.

JILL (V.O.)
(reasoning with herself)
We all make choices. That's what life is – one long series of choices.
(beat)
And I had choices. I could've gone to the beach ... I chose to walk the streets. I could've had a lobster dinner ... I chose pizza instead. I could've gone dancing with a babydyke. I chose not to.
(shrugs)
Which may have been the only smart choice I've made all day.
(beat; uncertainly)
I guess ...

Jill gets off the trash barrel and walks back to the Dreamgirl's car.

JILL
(continuing; out loud)
Ah, me. Well, if we're meant to be, it'll happen.
(to the car)
Right? So, when she comes for you, tell her I've gone to the Pied to try and salvage what's left of this evening. Thanks.

She pats the hood and leaves.

INT. THE PIED PIPER

Laura and Leslie are dancing. As one SONG ("LADIES NIGHT"/Kool and the Gang) is ending, Leslie grabs Laura's hand to lead her off the dance floor.

LAURA
Oh – not yet!

LESLIE
Let's go outside and neck!

Another song ("WE ARE FAMILY"/Sister Sledge) begins. They have to shout over the music.

LAURA
No – listen! It's the first song we ever danced to.

LESLIE
You must be thinking of someone else.

LAURA
(embarrassed)
Oh. That's right -- I'm sorry -- that was Helen.

LESLIE
(smiling)
See?

LAURA
(grabbing Leslie)
Then we'll make it our song -- come on!

They continue dancing.

EXT. THE DECK OUTSIDE THE PIED PIPER

"WE ARE FAMILY" CONTINUES. The Dreamgirl, her shoes in her hand, goes down the steps off the deck and walks away down the beach.

EXT. IN THE WELL-LIT ALLEY OUTSIDE THE PIED PIPER

"WE ARE FAMILY" is still PLAYING inside. As Jill approaches the door, the two Jogging Women are in front of her. The Other Jogging Woman is paying the cover charge while One Jogging Woman complains to the Doorperson.

ONE JOGGING WOMAN
How can you charge when there's no live entertainment?

OTHER JOGGING WOMAN
(handing over the money)
Oh, it doesn't matter.

ONE JOGGING WOMAN
(reading the sign)
"DISCOMANIA." Drag shows and disco, drag shows and disco --
whatever happened to culture in this town?

The Doorperson, looking very intimidating, takes a towel off the back of the chair by the door and twists it.

DOORPERSON
I strangled it with my bare hands.

ONE JOGGING WOMAN
(not intimidated)
I can believe it.

Another SONG ("LOVE TO LOVE YOU BABY"/Donna Summer) begins.

OTHER JOGGING WOMAN
(to One Jogging Woman)
Oh, come on -- I want to dance to this.

The Other Jogging Woman steers One Jogging Woman into the bar, as she protests.

> ONE JOGGING WOMAN
> Ooh – I hate Donna Summer.

Jill comes up to the Doorperson, who is shaking her head.

> JILL
> How's it going?

> DOORPERSON
> "It's not an adventure, it's just a job." Or so they say.

Jill gives the Doorperson the cover charge.

> JILL
> (barely hopeful)
> I wonder if you've seen someone. She's about this high -- I guess.
> (explaining)
> Well, I haven't actually seen her standing up ... but, uh – she's beautiful – uh, she's --

The Doorperson looks patiently bored. Jill realizes she's making no sense.

> JILL
> (continuing)
> – oh, forget it.

> DOORPERSON
> (agreeably)
> Okay.

Laura and Leslie are coming out the door just as Jill is going in.

> LAURA
> Oh, not again!

Leslie puts her arms around Jill's and Laura's shoulders.

> LESLIE
> (to Laura and Jill)
> Face it, kids, we're just three ships passing in the night.
> (looking for the Babydyke; to Jill)
> Lose your date? Or is it past her bedtime?

Jill gives her a dirty look.

> LAURA
> (to Jill)
> What about your Dreamgirl?

> JILL
> (resigned)
> She never came back.

> LAURA/LESLIE (together)
> Aawww ...

Julia Willis

                              JILL
I guess you haven't seen her inside.

                             LAURA
No.

                             LESLIE
But Laura only has eyes for me tonight.

                             LAURA
That's true.
                            (to Jill)
Is there anything we can do?

                              JILL
No ... I'll just have a drink and come back to the room. In an
hour or so ... unless you two have plans.

                             LESLIE
Come whenever you feel like it.

                             LAURA
Our home is your home. We'll leave the door unlocked.

                              JILL
Thanks, Mom.

                             LAURA
Do you want us to stay?

                              JILL
No, no – that's all right.

                             LAURA
Well –

                             LESLIE
See you in a while, then.

Laura and Leslie start down the alley. Jill calls after them.

                              JILL
I'm really okay!
                       (to the Doorperson)
I'm fine.

                          DOORPERSON
                           (not fooled)
Yeah, I can see that.

Jill goes into the bar.

EXT. COMMERCIAL STREET - LONG SHOT - THE DREAMGIRL

"LOVE TO LOVE YOU BABY" CONTINUES as the Dreamgirl comes off the
beach. The street is almost deserted. She puts her shoes on and walks
slowly in the direction of her car.

INT. THE PIED PIPER

"LOVE TO LOVE YOU BABY" CONTINUES as Jill goes over and asks the BARTENDER for a drink.

> JILL
> (to the Bartender)
> Soda. With a twist.

She notices the Babydyke at the end of the bar with a glass of beer, and she goes over. If she's hurt the girl's feelings, she wants to apologize.

> JILL
> (to the Babydyke)
> Well, I guess I was wrong.

The Babydyke just glares at her.

> JILL
> (continuing)
> I mean, you must be twenty-one to get in here, right?

The Babydyke continues to glare. The Bartender puts Jill's soda in front of her. Jill pays for it as she keeps on talking to the Babydyke.

> JILL
> (to the Bartender)
> Thanks.
> (to the Babydyke)
> Look, I just hope I haven't ruined your evening, and you won't take what I said too personally . . . see, I've been having sort of a rough time today --

The Babydyke throws her beer in Jill's face, gets off her barstool, and walks away. The Bartender hands Jill a pile of napkins.

> JILL
> (to the Bartender)
> Thanks.

EXT. COMMERCIAL STREET

Laura and Leslie are strolling slowly back to the guesthouse. The two Jogging Women come charging past them on the sidewalk. They are both shouting at the top of their lungs.

> ONE JOGGING WOMAN
> WHO WAS SHE?

> OTHER JOGGING WOMAN
> I TOLD YOU! SHE'S AN OLD FRIEND!

> ONE JOGGING WOMAN
> WHAT KIND OF "OLD FRIEND?"

Julia Willis

OTHER JOGGING WOMAN
A *FRIENDLY* OLD FRIEND!

ONE JOGGING WOMAN
I SAW THE WAY SHE WAS LOOKING AT YOU – AND IT WAS *NOT* JUST FRIENDLY!

OTHER JOGGING WOMAN
THAT'S RIDICULOUS – WHERE DO YOU GET THESE IDEAS?

ONE JOGGING WOMAN
WHERE ARE YOU GOING?

OTHER JOGGING WOMAN
I DON'T KNOW! LEAVE ME ALONE!

ONE JOGGING WOMAN
I'LL LEAVE YOU ALONE! I'LL LEAVE AND DRIVE BACK TONIGHT!

OTHER JOGGING WOMAN
GO AHEAD! I DON'T GIVE A SHIT!

Their AD LIB voices trail off down the street. Laura and Leslie try to regain their romantic composure.

LESLIE
Did you hear something?

LAURA
No, not a thing.

LESLIE
Must've been the wind.

They continue their stroll.

EXT. THE DECK OUTSIDE THE PIED PIPER - CLOSE SHOT - JILL

"THE HUSTLE" (Van McCoy) is playing inside. Jill has come out on the deck to recover her own composure and dry off. She is still wiping her face and clothes with a napkin and holding her soda in her other hand.

There is no one else on the deck, so Jill assumes she's alone.

JILL
(speaking to the sky)
Okay, girls. Just to show you my faith in the goddess is still intact, I'm going to make one more wish ... on that star ... that one there, the little yellow one.

She closes her eyes and makes her wish. A VOICE comes from below the railing.

VOICE (O.S.)
Psst! Jill!

Jill opens her eyes, startled. For an instant she thinks she's getting a message from The Great Beyond.

                                        JILL
                                   (looking up)
Yeah?

                                     VOICE (O.S.)
Over here!

THE DECK

Jill looks toward the steps to the beach and sees Martha hiding there. She
is both relieved and disappointed to find it's only Martha.

                                        JILL
Oh – what are you doing down there?

                                       MARTHA
Come here – hurry!

Jill goes over and crouches down with Martha, who is further embroiled in
a web of intrigue.

                                       MARTHA
                                  (full of drama)
You've got to help me. Have you seen Kate?

                                        JILL
I don't know. I just got here.

                                       MARTHA
She was supposed to meet me here half an hour ago. You know
Kate, don't you?

                                        JILL
Uh – do I? I'm not sure.

                                       MARTHA
                                 (describing Kate)
About my height? Short curly hair? Thirtyish? Therapist?
                                      (beat)
Haven't seen her?

                                        JILL
Haven't, no ... I think.

                                       MARTHA
                               (worried but excited)
Something's gone wrong. She should've been here by now.
                                 (confiding in Jill)
Fran *knows*.

                                        JILL
About you and Kate?

                                       MARTHA
No – about me and Nancy.

JILL

Who's Nancy?

MARTHA

I *told* you – Kate's old lover that Fran and I are living with.

JILL
(confused)

Oh.

MARTHA

Nancy found out that Kate was coming to see *me*, and so she told Fran about *us*.

JILL

About you and Kate?

MARTHA
(thinking Jill is pretty dense)

No! About me and *Nancy*.

JILL
(barely following her)

Oh – that's right.

MARTHA

Now Fran's looking for us.

JILL
(sure she's got it straight this time)

For you and Nancy.

MARTHA

No! For me and Kate! Jesus.

Martha is becoming exasperated with Jill. Jill isn't crazy about Martha's histrionics, either, and tries to change the subject.

JILL
(looking out to sea)

My – isn't the ocean calm tonight?

MARTHA
(paying no attention)

Is Fran inside?

JILL

I don't know Fran.

MARTHA

Really? She knows you.

Jill stands up, weary of all this drama.

JILL

Well, if she asks me, I guess I haven't seen you.

Martha stands up, too, on the steps.

MARTHA
No! You haven't seen me. Or Kate.

JILL
No, I haven't seen Kate ... I guess.

MARTHA
Or Nancy.

JILL
I don't know Nancy.

MARTHA
Sure?
(describing Nancy)
About my height, short curly hair –

JILL
(pretending)
Oh, sure – Nancy.

MARTHA
Remember, you haven't seen her.

JILL
I haven't seen anybody. All evening.

MARTHA
Good, good – stick to that.
(beat)
I gotta go.

Martha creeps back down the steps.

CLOSE SHOT - JILL

Looking up at the sky again, she sighs.

JILL
So much for wishes.

MARTHA (O.S.)
(stage whisper)
Psst! Jill!

Jill leans over the railing.

JILL
Yes, Martha?

MARTHA (O.S.)
Ssh! Don't say my name. Listen, if you see Kate – can you hear me?

                         JILL
                      (repeating)
If I see Kate --

                      MARTHA (O.S.)
Ssh! Anyone up there with you?

                         JILL
                    (looking around)
No.

                      MARTHA (O.S.)
Okay -- if you see Kate, tell her: "Plan B."

                         JILL
Plan B.

                      MARTHA (O.S.)
Ssh! Just tell her . . . okay?

                         JILL
Okay.

                      MARTHA (O.S.)
Thanks.

                         JILL
Okay.
                     (to herself)
Plan B.

                      MARTHA (O.S.)
SSH!

Jill backs away from the railing.

EXT. COMMERCIAL STREET NEAR THE DREAMGIRL'S PARKED CAR

Laura and Leslie are still strolling along. They've been talking about their relationship, as Laura finishes her thought.

                        LAURA
-- and that's why we're so lucky.

                        LESLIE
Yes, we are, my love.

ON THE CORNER - LAURA AND LESLIE

They reach the corner -- and there, down the side street, is the Dreamgirl, standing by her car, keys in her hand, gazing solemnly into a shop window.

They stop dead in their tracks. Laura is very excited, while Leslie tries to remain calm.

                        LAURA
Look -- it's her!

Once Upon a Dream

LESLIE
Ssh!

LAURA
But it *must* be – Jill's Dreamgirl! Mustn't it?

LESLIE
Yeah, I think so, but wait –

Laura is dying to run right up to her.

LAURA
No, no, we have to meet her -- we have to take her to Jill.

LESLIE
Laura, we can't just go up and grab her. We have to think of a way to approach her.

LAURA
(rehearsing)
"Good evening. We've come to take you to Jill."

She tries to go forward, but Leslie holds her back.

LESLIE
Yeah, right – "she's waiting for you in the Emerald City. I'm Toto and this is my lover Tinkerbelle." Come on -- we don't want to scare her off.

DOWN THE SIDE STREET - THE DREAMGIRL

Meanwhile, the Dreamgirl has stopped looking in the shop window. She glances at Laura and Leslie curiously and then goes around to the driver's side of her car. She unlocks the door to get in.

BACK TO THE CORNER

Laura sees her at the car and panics.

LAURA
Oh – she's leaving!
(shouting)
Wait, stop – please don't go!

LESLIE
Laura, no, don't --

Leslie can't keep Laura from running toward the Dreamgirl, so she follows.

THE DREAMGIRL'S P.O.V.

She watches Laura and Leslie approach.

REVERSE P.O.V.

We DOLLY along with Laura and Leslie as they watch *her* watching *them*.

EXT. THE DREAMGIRL'S PARKED CAR

When they reach her, Laura and Leslie are nervously out of breath. The Dreamgirl isn't afraid of them, but she is somewhat puzzled by their odd behavior and vaguely suspicious, keeping her hand on the car door. When she speaks, she has a slight French-Canadian accent.

> DREAMGIRL
> Yes? May I help you?

Now that she's really talking to the Dreamgirl, Laura doesn't know what to say.

> LAURA
> Hi. Uh . . .
> (passing the buck; to Leslie)
> You tell her.

> LESLIE
> Thanks a lot.
> (to the Dreamgirl)
> Hello.

> DREAMGIRL
> Hello.

> LESLIE
> Uh – my name is Leslie . . . Leslie McGee.

Leslie puts out her hand -- the Dreamgirl takes her hand off the door handle and politely shakes it.

> DREAMGIRL
> I am Jackie LeFleur.

> LAURA
> And I'm Laura Battaglia.

She shakes hands with the Dreamgirl, too.

> DREAMGIRL
> How do you do?

> LAURA
> Oh, fine, fine -- I do fine.
> (throwing it back to Leslie)
> Go ahead.

> LESLIE
> Well, we were driving down this afternoon – Laura and I – on Route Six, and uh – we noticed you . . . well, that is, we noticed your car.

> DREAMGIRL
> Yes?

Once Upon a Dream   79

LAURA

Yes, you passed us. You must've been going eighty. We were in an old Volvo.
                    (back to Leslie)
Go on.

LESLIE

It's a beautiful car – yours, I mean.

DREAMGIRL

Yes. Thank you.
                    (beat)
I'm sorry, but it's not for sale.

LAURA

Oh, no, we don't want your car -- we want you!
                    (back to Leslie)
I'm sorry, go ahead.

Leslie gives Laura a look that could kill. The Dreamgirl rests her hand back on the door handle. Leslie tries to explain.

LESLIE

What Laura means is – uh – that makes it sound like we're looking for a threesome ... and we're not.

LAURA

No, that's not what I –

LESLIE

No. Uh – we're a couple ...

LAURA

And we have our friend Jill with us. Only she's not a threesome either.
                    (back to Leslie)
You explain it.

LESLIE
                    (between her teeth)
Thank you, darling.
                    (to the Dreamgirl)
Well, the thing is ... there's a friend of ours who would love to meet you ... and we thought that if you'd like to meet *her*, we could tell her where you're staying, or vice versa --

LAURA

Good, good.

LESLIE
                    (continuing)
-- and tomorrow you might want to get together for brunch or – something.

---

80   Julia Willis

                    LAURA
                  (to Leslie)
Great idea.
                (to the Dreamgirl)
She's a wonderful person. I'm sure you'd like her. A lot.

                  DREAMGIRL
                  (reserved)
Perhaps ... but I'm afraid it won't be possible.

Laura realizes the Dreamgirl may be going away tonight.

                    LAURA
Oh – you're not leaving, are you?

                  DREAMGIRL
Yes, I'm driving on to Boston tonight.

                    LAURA
                  (horrified)
Oh, but you can't! Not at night!

                  DREAMGIRL
Why not?

                    LAURA
                (thinking quick)
Well, it's very dangerous!
                  (to Leslie)
Tell her why it's so dangerous.

                   LESLIE
                   (stuck)
Uh – the roads. The curves. Drunk drivers.

                    LAURA
And skunks.

                   LESLIE
What?

                    LAURA
Skunks.
               (to the Dreamgirl)
They're all over the road at night. In packs.

                   LESLIE
Packs?

                    LAURA
Very dangerous. You should wait and meet Jill and go tomorrow.
Avoid the skunks.

The Dreamgirl is amused but determined to go.

Once Upon a Dream

                    DREAMGIRL
I'm sorry I can't meet your friend, but I have no place to stay the
night ... and I don't think I would be such good company, anyway.
                    (beat; wistful)
You see ... well, maybe you will think I'm a little bit crazy, but I
came here today looking for someone. Someone special.
                    (beat)
I guess that does sound ... crazy, yes?

                    LAURA
No, no.

                    LESLIE
Not at all.

                    DREAMGIRL
I'm glad you don't think so. But now I don't know what to think.
It was as if a strong magnet drew me here ... you see? And here
I am ... but nothing happens. And when you *know* a thing in your
heart and it doesn't happen, you feel foolish.
                    (beat)
So -- that's how I feel ... and that's why I must go now.

Laura and Leslie protest.

                    LAURA
Oh, no -- you can't.

                    LESLIE
Sometimes these things take a little time.

                    LAURA
That's right.
                    (pointing to Leslie)
We didn't meet for twenty-eight years.

                    LESLIE
                    (to Laura)
That's not quite what I meant, dear.

                    DREAMGIRL
You're very understanding, but I really don't know --

                    LAURA
Please stay until tomorrow.

                    DREAMGIRL
But it's so late, and I don't have a room --

ANGLE ON LAURA AND LESLIE

They stare briefly at the Dreamgirl and then exchange a look.

EXT. IN THE WELL-LIT ALLEY OUTSIDE THE PIED PIPER

"I WILL SURVIVE" (Gloria Gaynor) is playing inside. Jill comes out of the bar. She's ready to call it a night. FRAN (who actually *is* about Martha's height, "short curly hair, thirtyish, therapist") is talking to the Doorperson, who nods (like a therapist).

FRAN
(bitter)
She lied to me – it was all lies!

Jill starts to walk past them without speaking.

DOORPERSON
(doing her job; to Jill)

Good night.

JILL

Good night.

Fran sees Jill.

FRAN

Jill!

Jill turns and sees Fran. Fran obviously knows her, but Jill doesn't recognize Fran.

JILL
(blankly)

Oh. Hi.

FRAN
What are you doing down here?

JILL

Oh, not much.

She is racking her brain, frantically trying to place Fran.

FRAN
You alone?

JILL

Not exactly ... I'm here with Laura and Leslie.

FRAN

Who?

JILL
Friends of mine. Maybe you haven't met them.

FRAN
(reading sex into it)

Oh ... *that* **kind of friends.**

Once Upon a Dream   83

                              JILL
                           (innocent)
No, just friends.
                             (beat)
Uh – how are things with you?

                              FRAN
Don't even ask.
                   (indicating the Doorperson)
I was just telling Barbara what a fucking mess my life is right now.

                              JILL
                            (polite)
Really.

                              FRAN
You haven't seen Martha around, have you?

Jill brightens. Now she thinks she knows who she's talking to.

                              JILL
Martha. Sure -- I just saw her out on the beach.

                              FRAN
You did?

                              JILL
Yeah. And she said to tell you: "Plan B."

                              FRAN
                           (puzzled)
Plan what?

                              JILL
                       (repeating herself)
"Plan B?"

Jill has jumped to the conclusion that she's talking to *Kate*. Now she realizes
her mistake.

                              FRAN
                        (smelling a rat)
That's no message for me – that's probably for Kate.
                             (beat)
Don't you know who I am?

The Doorperson standing behind Fran is mouthing the name "Fran" for Jill
to see. Jill does.

                              JILL
Oh, sure I do, Fran. I know *you*. I guess I'm confusing *Martha*
with someone else.

                              FRAN
Did you see her or not?

JILL

Uh, no -- uh -- I think that was Millie I saw, not Martha. Both *Ms*, you know -- Millie, Martha -- uh, been a long day, and I just --

FRAN
(fed up)

God, you're all liars.

Fran storms into the bar.

JILL
(to the Doorperson)

Thanks, anyway.

DOORPERSON
(kindly but cynical)

You don't belong in P-Town, honey.

JILL

No, I guess not.

EXT. A SIDE STREET OFF COMMERCIAL STREET - LATE NIGHT

The Dreamgirl's car is still parked in the same spot. The two Jogging Women are passing it, walking slowly, holding hands, making up their differences -- in other words, processing.

ONE JOGGING WOMAN
If we could only resolve our intimacy issues --

OTHER JOGGING WOMAN
But you can't put too much pressure on the relationship. That's what's causing all these explosions.

ONE JOGGING WOMAN
I just want everything to be perfect.

OTHER JOGGING WOMAN
It can't be perfect. We're only human.

Jill comes up to the car as the Jogging Women pass her, going in the opposite direction.

ONE JOGGING WOMAN
I feel like this is all my fault.

OTHER JOGGING WOMAN
You don't need to feel guilty.

ONE JOGGING WOMAN
Let's go back to the room. I need for you to hold me.

They go quietly down the street. Jill, lost in her own thoughts, stands by the car, talking to it.

JILL

Hi. Me again. Just thought I'd drop by to say good night. If you need a blanket or a cup of hot oil or anything, I'm at Lady Jane's Inn. Number seven. Nighty-night, sweet dreams, don't let the bedbugs bite.

She leans over and kisses the top of the car and walks away.

EXT. COMMERCIAL STREET - LATE NIGHT - LONG SHOT

The street is empty now, and the fog is rolling in. Jill walks alone, thinking.

JILL (V.O.)

It could have worked out ... I just know it. My body has never lied to me. I know magic when I feel it ... it's fate. Why would I have this feeling if we weren't meant to be together? We are ... we are ...

DISSOLVE TO:

INT. ROOM NUMBER SEVEN (JILL'S FANTASY) - NIGHT

Jill enters the room. Laura and Leslie must be asleep. The Dreamgirl is sitting up in Jill's bed, naked from the waist up and bathed in the glow of a soft amber light (like firelight).

Jill is not overly surprised to see her there because after all, it *is* fate. The Dreamgirl smiles.

DREAMGIRL

Hello.

JILL
(smiling back)

Hello.

DREAMGIRL

I hope you don't mind finding me in your bed like this.

JILL
(so calm; so cool)

Not at all.

DREAMGIRL

Your friends said it would be all right.

JILL

It's fine.

Jill takes her clothes off quickly and easily and comes over to sit on the bed. The Dreamgirl cups Jill's breast in her hand.

DREAMGIRL

You are even lovelier than I knew you would be.

JILL

So are you.

Julia Willis

DREAMGIRL
I feel as if I have known you for a long, long time. Forever.

JILL
You have. I am your destiny.

Jill pulls back the covers to reveal the rest of the Dreamgirl's body. She leans over and lightly kisses the Dreamgirl between her legs. The Dreamgirl takes Jill's hand, grips it tightly, and rolls her over onto the bed.

Effortlessly, as though they've been doing it lifetime after lifetime throughout all eternity, they make love. Their mutual pleasure is exquisite and their timing impeccable. They even have simultaneous orgasms. It is all perfect.

CUT TO:

EXT. THE GUESTHOUSE - CLOSE SHOT - JILL

Jill arrives at the guesthouse, still talking to herself.

JILL (V.O.)
(her soliloquy)
We are ... I know we are. I mean, what's body chemistry for if you can't *do* anything with it?

She is passing room number eight. One of the Jogging Women, in the heat of passion, is making a lot of noise inside.

ONE JOGGING WOMAN (O.S.)
Oh God! Oh God! Oh God!

Jill stops for a moment to listen.

ONE JOGGING WOMAN (O.S.)
(continuing)
Oh God! Oh God! Oh God!

JILL
(to herself; out loud)
I guess they're through processing.

OUTSIDE ROOM NUMBER SEVEN

Jill goes on to the door of number seven. She stands outside, knowing if she goes in it will mean the evening is over and she's failed to find the Dreamgirl or even a reasonable facsimile of one and she'll once again be sleeping alone.

After a moment's hesitation, she sits on the bench between rooms seven and eight.

JILL (V.O.)
(musing)
I wonder if Laura's still awake.
(beat)
I should've brought something to read.
(MORE)

Once Upon a Dream

JILL (cont'd)
(another beat)
Oh, I might as well face it -- destiny, fate, it's all a bunch of crap!
I set up these impossible goals, and I end up with nothing. And
nobody ... I've just got to learn to be more realistic ...

DISSOLVE TO:

INT. ROOM NUMBER SEVEN (JILL'S FANTASY) - NIGHT

Jill enters the room. Laura and Leslie must be asleep. The Biker, the
Babydyke, and Martha are all sitting in Jill's bed, bathed in a garish red glow.
They are all licking their chops, ready to eat her alive.

BIKER
Hi, Jill.

BABYDYKE
Come on in.

MARTHA
We've been waiting for you.

Jill, terrified, turns and lunges for the door. She tries to open it, but it's locked.

BABYDYKE
Come on, Jill.

BIKER
We won't hurt you.

MARTHA
Destiny calls.

They all begin to laugh maniacally.

ANGLE ON JILL

Jill desperately tugs at the door, but it won't budge. She's trapped!

QUICK CUT TO:

EXT. OUTSIDE ROOM NUMBER SEVEN - LATE NIGHT

Jill jolts out of that fantasy, relieved but shaken.

JILL
Maybe not *that* realistic.

She gets up off the bench and goes back to the door of room number seven.

JILL (V.O.)
(continuing)
Okay -- no more fantasies.

Julia Willis

She puts her hand on the doorknob.

>   JILL (V.O.)
>   (continuing)
>   Maybe Leslie brought something to read.

She opens the door.

INT. ROOM NUMBER SEVEN

Jill enters the room. Laura and Leslie must be asleep. Exactly the way Jill pictured her in the fantasy, the Dreamgirl is sitting up in Jill's bed, naked to the waist and bathed in the glow of a soft amber light.

Unlike her fantasy counterpart, Jill is completely astonished. The Dreamgirl, on the other hand, knows immediately, instinctively, that Jill is that special someone she has been looking for.

>   DREAMGIRL
>   (smiling)
>   Hello.

>   JILL
>   (dumbfounded)
>   Uh -- uh --

She cannot believe this is really happening. She blinks hard. The Dreamgirl is still there.

>   DREAMGIRL
>   (just as in the fantasy)
>   I hope you don't mind finding me in your bed like this.

>   JILL
>   Uh -- mind?

She is speechless -- the Dreamgirl even says her fantasy lines perfectly.

>   DREAMGIRL
>   Your friends said it would be all right.

This is too much for Jill.

>   JILL
>   Uh -- would you excuse me for a minute?

>   DREAMGIRL
>   Yeah, sure.

Jill rushes into the bathroom and closes the door. The Dreamgirl looks at the closed door calmly, though she does find Jill's behavior a bit odd.

INT. BATHROOM/ROOM NUMBER SEVEN - CLOSE SHOT - JILL

Jill turns on the tap and splashes cold water on her face. She looks in the mirror . . . is she dreaming? She pinches her cheek . . . it hurts. This is *real*.

She glances toward the room and the Dreamgirl in amazement, briefly checks herself out in the mirror, and turns to go and meet her destiny.

Then she stops, comes back to the mirror, checks her face for pimples or dirt, checks for food between her teeth, checks her breath, and fluffs her hair. Now she's ready. Still very nervous, but ready.

INT. ROOM NUMBER SEVEN - TWO SHOT - JILL AND THE DREAMGIRL

Laura and Leslie are presumably still asleep. The Dreamgirl is still sitting up in Jill's bed. Jill comes out of the bathroom and over to the bed.

JILL
(shy)

Hi.

DREAMGIRL

Are you all right?

JILL

I'm -- wonderful. Um -- I'm Jill.

DREAMGIRL
(introducing herself)

Jackie.

(beat)

I hope I'm not imposing, but your friends said you wouldn't mind. They're very nice.

JILL

They're -- wonderful.

The Dreamgirl laughs.

DREAMGIRL

Is *everything* wonderful?

JILL

It is now.

Jill sits gently on the edge of the bed.

JILL
(continuing)

That is -- I hope this doesn't sound crazy, but I've been looking for you all day.

DREAMGIRL

I know. They told me.

JILL
(embarrassed)

Oh.

                              DREAMGIRL
I don't think you're crazy.

                                JILL
                              (relieved)
Oh. Good.

                              DREAMGIRL
I think you're lovely.

This is too good to be true. Jill doesn't know how to reply.

                                JILL
Oh. Um –

The Dreamgirl takes her hand.

                              DREAMGIRL
And I hope this doesn't sound crazy to *you*, but I think I've been
looking for you all my life.

                                JILL
For me? Really?

The Dreamgirl nods and kisses Jill's hand. Jill sighs.

                              DREAMGIRL
I can't explain it . . . I just know it.

                                JILL
I know. And I just feel it.

                              DREAMGIRL
Then it must be right.

                                JILL
Destiny.

Jill leans forward to kiss the Dreamgirl. Through the thin walls, the passionate
cries of the Other Jogging Woman interrupt.

                    OTHER JOGGING WOMAN (O.S.)
          Oh yes! Oh God! OH YES! OH GOD!

Jill groans and stops. The Dreamgirl smiles.

                              DREAMGIRL
It's all right. Come here.

She unbuttons Jill's shirt and buries her head between Jill's breasts. Jill moans.
The Other Jogging Woman continues.

                    OTHER JOGGING WOMAN (O.S.)
                              (quickly)
     Oh God, oh God, oh God, oh God, oh God, oh God – OH GOD!

It is all too apparent that the Other Jogging Woman has had her orgasm.
Jill and the Dreamgirl laugh softly. This breaks the ice.

                              JILL
                          (confessing)
I'm afraid I'm a little nervous.

                           DREAMGIRL
So am I.

Jill crawls into bed and takes the Dreamgirl in her arms.

                              JILL
What would you like me to do?

                           DREAMGIRL
                           (simply)
Use your imagination.

They kiss long and tenderly.

                                          SLOW DISSOLVE TO:

EXT. THE GUESTHOUSE - MORNING

Laura and Leslie are loading the Volvo to go home.

                             LAURA
Oh, I wish you didn't have that meeting.

                             LESLIE
So do I. I wish we could stay a week.

                             LAURA
I know ... but it was nice. I'm so glad we came.

                             LESLIE
I think Jill's glad, too.

They stand together, looking at the closed door to room number seven.

                             LAURA
Yeah ...
                            (beat)
You're sure she's getting a ride back?

                             LESLIE
If she isn't, she can just float home. On the wings of angels.

                             LAURA
                           (singing)
"Ah, sweet mystery of life –"

                             LESLIE
                          (joining in)
"– at last I've found you."

They shush one another and start to get in the car.

                             LAURA
Leslie?

LESLIE

Hmm?

LAURA

Were you awake last night? When Jill came home?

Leslie considers her answer carefully.

LESLIE
(lying)

No.

LAURA
(also lying)

I wasn't either.

As they get in the Volvo, the two Jogging Women come out of room number eight. They are back to their old selves.

OTHER JOGGING WOMAN

I don't *want* any coffee!

ONE JOGGING WOMAN

Then don't *have* any!

OTHER JOGGING WOMAN

Why do we have to drive?

ONE JOGGING WOMAN

Because they stop serving breakfast in five minutes, that's why.

INT. LESLIE'S CAR

Leslie starts her car, and on the RADIO Handel's "MESSIAH" is PLAYING.

EXT. OUTSIDE ROOM NUMBER EIGHT

As One Jogging Woman gets in on the driver's side of her car, she remembers something.

ONE JOGGING WOMAN

Do you have the key?

OTHER JOGGING WOMAN

No – don't you?

ONE JOGGING WOMAN
(furious)

Ooh, you – get in the car!

OTHER JOGGING WOMAN

Don't you yell at me!

ONE JOGGING WOMAN

GET IN THE CAR!

The Other Jogging Woman gets in.

EXT. THE GUESTHOUSE - LONG SHOT

The two cars (Leslie's Volvo and the Jogging Woman's Subaru) drive away with the "MESSIAH" still PLAYING. Then the CAMERA PANS RIGHT to the door of room number seven.

ANGLE ON DOORKNOB - MED. SHOT

Jill's hand reaches around the door and puts the "DO NOT DISTURB" sign on the doorknob. The Dreamgirl's hand appears, covers Jill's hand, and both hands slide back around the door which closes, softly.

CLOSEUP - "DO NOT DISTURB" SIGN

as the "HALLELUJAH CHORUS" SWELLS and we

FADE OUT.

THE END

Amazon X

FADE IN:

EXT. BEHIND A MODERN NEW ENGLAND COURTHOUSE (LATE SPRING) - AFTERNOON - LONG SHOT

The back of a cold brick building -- no windows. BONGO MUSIC. We SEE TWO POLICEMEN come around the left side of the building half-running, hands on their holsters, their eyes frantically scanning the horizon.

As the camera PANS to the right, following them, an empty police cruiser looms up in the f.g. -- crouched down behind the cruiser is the ESCAPEE, a woman in a gray jumpsuit with a pink sweater covering the prison lettering on the front and back. There is a police revolver in her hand.

She breathes hard, watching the progress of the cops and looking for a way out. As the two cops continue around the building, searching under cars and in dumpsters, she conceals her weapon and makes a break, walking briskly in the opposite direction.

EXT. JUNE AND NANCY'S HOUSE - AFTERNOON - ESTABLISHING

Bongos STOP and MUSIC ("MY LITTLE CORNER OF THE WORLD" as it was recorded in the 60s by Anita Bryant) BEGINS as we go from the stony exterior of the courthouse to a bungalow exuding a cozy warmth.

The front porch is full of plants and has a porch swing with pillows and a big straw welcome mat with the outline of a labyris on it.

TITLES BEGIN

INT. JUNE AND NANCY'S HOUSE

The SONG CONTINUES, and the CAMERA MOVES around the house, subtly revealing who the occupants are (two YULPs - Young Urban Lesbian Professionals) and the state of their relationship (past and present). In the living room: Nancy's desk piled high with legal work from the office, and a framed poster of a Lily Tomlin show.

Down the hall in the bedroom: a framed poster from the movie "THERESE AND ISABELLE," June's desk piled high with grant proposals and books on the homeless, and an art deco dresser with photos of friends and family stuck in the mirror along one side and a series of photos of June and Nancy down the other side.

June and Nancy's photos go from grinning wildly (on an early honeymoon trip) to smiling happily (on a later vacation) to sitting together in a group of women (at a party) with Nancy looking the other way. A fourth picture lying out on the dresser is of the two of them on the front porch of their house, alone together -- Nancy in the swing, reading, and June watering the plants.

Back down the hall in the bathroom: a shower curtain covered with the names of famous lesbians, and above the toilet a framed picture of Sigourney Weaver from the movie "ALIEN." On the bathroom mirror a message is scrawled in soap: "WE NEED TO TALK!" It has been there for several days.

As we come BACK to the living room and move through an archway into the kitchen, the END OF THE SONG is interrupted by a RADIO news bulletin.

END TITLES

INT. JUNE AND NANCY'S KITCHEN

During the bulletin the CAMERA WANDERS into the kitchen, looking at the flyers and signs on the refrigerator door, the herbal tea packages, and other kitchen details. Breakfast dishes are still in the sink. The back door is open.

                              D.J. (V.O.)
Uh -- we switch you now to our newsroom for this late-breaking story. Gail?

The D.J. voice is superseded by the NEWSCASTER with a TELETYPE running UNDER.

                          NEWSCASTER (V.O.)
                         (nervous and rushed)
Thank you, Jeff. Good afternoon. I'm Gail Huppermeyer with this -- uh -- late-breaking story.
                           (reading copy)
Within the hour, Linda Bradley, a young Somerville woman arraigned today on attempted murder charges stemming from the alleged shooting of her husband, has escaped from police custody and is presently at large. She apparently made her escape from a holding room in the Middlesex County Courthouse by disarming an officer and making her getaway through a service entrance, and was last seen wearing gray coveralls and a pink sweater. She is to be considered armed and dangerous. If you see this woman, do not attempt to apprehend her, but notify police immediately.
                              (beat)
We'll have more details on this story as it progresses in our newscast on the hour. This is Gail Huppermeyer returning you now to Jeff Conway and more music.

The TELETYPE STOPS.

                              D.J. (V.O.)
Thanks, Gail -- quite a story, And we'll be back with more drive-time oldies right after this.

A commercial for a local jewelry store begins, with "OVER THE RAINBOW" performed by Mantovani UNDER. The VOICEOVER is one of those untrained voices reading ad copy.

                          SANDI LEE (V.O.)
                        (unbearably nasal)
Hi. I'm Sandi Lee, for Louie Lee Jewelers of Medford, and I believe in love. And when my dad tells me to slash our already low price on our one-carat diamond engagement rings, I do it.

Through the open back door JUNE enters with an empty trash bucket. She's been outside putting the trash in the alley and didn't hear the newsflash. She is still dressed in her clothes from work -- a sweater and slacks.

> SANDI LEE (V.O.)
> (continuing)
> I slash and I slash until prices are cut to the bone and just right for you, our customers . . . because I believe in love, and I know you do, too.
> (beat)
> So stop by and see me, Sandi Lee, or my brother Tod, at Louie Lee Jewelers of Medford, and let us show you what diamonds and love are all about. That's Louie Lee Jewelers of --

June switches off the radio on the kitchen counter.

> JUNE
> (imitating Sandi)
> -- Medford. The hottest rocks at the coolest prices."

She looks around the kitchen for other things that need doing. She begins to run water in the sink and hum "OVER THE RAINBOW." In the living room a DOOR SLAMS.

> JUNE
> (continuing)
> That you?

INT. JUNE AND NANCY'S LIVING ROOM

NANCY has just come from work, more dressed up than June and carrying a briefcase.

> NANCY
> (responding)
> That me.

Nancy goes over to her desk in the corner, puts down her briefcase and picks up her mail. This is her house, but she doesn't act very comfortable in it.

> JUNE (O.S.)
> I tried to get you, but you'd already left.

> NANCY
> (guiltily)
> Oh.

June comes into the living room, wiping her hands on a dishtowel.

> JUNE
> (repeating herself)
> You'd already left.

She stops a few feet away from Nancy, who is not very approachable today. Nancy gives her an explanation before she asks for one.

> NANCY
> I left a little early -- I had some errands to run.

                    JUNE
        Okay. I'm not checking up on you.
Nancy puts down her mail.

                    NANCY
        I didn't say you were.

                    JUNE
                 (half-joking)
        Should I?
Nancy picks up her briefcase again.

                    NANCY
        I guess I'll go out and come in again.

                    JUNE
        Why don't you just kiss me instead?

Nancy puts down the briefcase and kisses June lightly.

                    NANCY
        How's that?

                    JUNE
        Preoccupied . . . bad day?

                    NANCY
        No, no -- not bad. Busy. Got my continuance.

                    JUNE
        Oh -- good. Sorry I missed you. I wanted you to pick up the pizza
        on your way home.
                 (beat)
        The pizza I called in. It was ready two minutes ago.

                    NANCY
                 (bored)
        Is that what we're having?

                    JUNE
        Yeah -- do you want to go get it?

                    NANCY
        Not really. I just walked in the door, and I've only got a half hour.
        Advocates' meeting tonight.
June sighs and holds out her hand.

                    JUNE
        Okay.

                    NANCY
        What?

                    JUNE
        Keys? You've got me blocked in -- right?

Julia Willis

Nancy doesn't want June to drive her car -- could she be hiding something in it?

> NANCY
>
> Oh. No, never mind -- I'll go.

> JUNE
>
> No, I'll go -- I just have to take your car.

> NANCY
> (hedging)
>
> No, no -- it's acting up a little. I'll go. What name?

> JUNE
>
> Yours. Half-pepperoni, half-mushroom.

> NANCY
>
> As usual. And why don't we find a pizza place that delivers?

> JUNE
>
> We did. Their pizzas suck . . . you need any money?

> NANCY
>
> Nope.

Nancy leaves. June reflects for a moment on their exchange. It wasn't what you'd call passionate -- it wasn't even particularly affectionate. They've been together for five years, living together for three.

> JUNE
> (shaking her head)
>
> Nope.
> (beat; to the door)
>
> Then what *do* you need?

She turns to go back into the kitchen, flipping on the TV as she goes by.

> JUNE
> (continuing)
>
> Or, better yet, what do *I* need?

June goes out. The CAMERA PANS OVER and LINGERS on the TV screen, as an ANCHORPERSON does a news tag.

> ANCHORPERSON
>
> -- and we'll take you to the courthouse where Ron Bonner is standing by with a live report. All this and more, as the search for Linda Bradley continues, on the Eyewitness Newshour.

Theme MUSIC up.

INT. JUNE AND NANCY'S KITCHEN

The TV in the b.g. DRONES on. June begins to set the table. Suddenly, there is a loud CRASH outside -- as if someone just backed their car into half a dozen trash cans at once.

                                  JUNE
    What the -- ?

She drops what she's doing and runs out the back door.

EXT. JUNE AND NANCY'S BACKYARD

June comes running out the door and looks toward the alley. We get her reaction before we can SEE what's happened.
                                  JUNE
    Oh my God!

The camera FOLLOWS June across the small backyard to

THE ALLEY

where a woman is lying on the ground with garbage cans strewn all around her. It is THE AMAZON FROM OUTER SPACE, fiat on her back, groaning. (And what do you know -- she is played by the same actress who is playing the part of Linda Bradley, Escapee.)

She wears a spacesuit similar to the prison jumpsuit the Escapee wears (though the fit is better, the color is different, and there are several odd markings on the sleeves and/or pockets to denote her rank -- there's also a patch with her starfleet logo on it, a circle with a dot in the middle), and there's a strange electronic object (sort of a cross between a beeper and a large watch) on her wrist.

But while Linda is a frightened woman (lacking in self-esteem, battered and abused by an alcoholic husband, and trapped in her life) running from the law, the Amazon is supremely confident, viewing Earth and its inhabitants as an anthropologist might study a tribe of savage headhunters. She doesn't look down on things condescendingly -- they just appear barbaric by her standards. She speaks English well (as if she learned it in school) and has a fairly good working knowledge of the culture, but there are gaps in her education.

So we would never mistake the Amazon for Linda the Escapee (though others will) -- they come from vastly different worlds. At the moment, however, the Amazon is stunned, with the wind knocked out of her, as June comes running to her aid.

                                  JUNE
    Are you all right?

The Amazon cannot reply. June looks around.

                                  JUNE
                              (continuing)
    What happened? Were you attacked?

The Amazon shakes her head.

Julia Willis

                              JUNE
                          (continuing)
No? Did you fall?

The Amazon nods, looking up at the sky.

                              JUNE
                          (continuing)
Oh -- you fell. Okay. Uh -- can you move? No, don't move -- stay
there. I'll call an ambulance.

The Amazon shakes her head and tries to sit up. June helps her.

                              JUNE
                          (continuing)
Careful now, careful -- easy -- where does it hurt? Can you tell
me? Can you talk?

The Amazon comes to a sitting position, but she still doesn't have her wind back.
She shakes her head. June takes this to mean she is hearing-impaired, and she
tries to talk to her ("Where does it hurt?") in sign language. The Amazon looks
blank.

                              JUNE
                          (continuing)
Isn't that right? Maybe I'm not doing it right -- I took the damn
course two years ago.

                            AMAZON
                        (gasping it out)
I'm -- all -- right.

                              JUNE
Oh. You *can* talk. Can you hear me, too?

                            AMAZON
                          (nodding)
Can -- you -- help -- me -- up?

                              JUNE
Sure, sure, if you're ready -- if you don't think anything's --

She helps the Amazon to her feet and checks her up and down. The Amazon
is several inches taller than June.

                              JUNE
How do you feel?

                            AMAZON
Where am I?

The Amazon looks around her, dazed.

                              JUNE
In my backyard. You fell . . . I don't see how, exactly . . .

_____

Amazon X   103

                         AMAZON
Yes. I fell.

                          JUNE
Maybe you better come inside . . . can you walk?

                         AMAZON
                    (looking at her legs)
Uh -- yes.

                          JUNE
Come on, then.

She helps the Amazon, who is wobbly on her feet, toward the back door.

EXT. AN ALLEY BEHIND A ROW OF STORES

To the accompaniment of more BONGO MUSIC, the Escapee runs into the alley
and boosts herself up and into a dumpster beside a loading dock. In the b.g.
a police cruiser slowly passes by.

EXT. A PHONE BOOTH OUTSIDE THE PIZZA PARLOR - LATE AFTERNOON
- MED. SHOT - NANCY

Nancy is on the phone, her back to the camera. Her car is parked next to the
phone booth, and a large pizza box is sitting on the hood. In the b.g. is the
pizza parlor, with the "TONY'S PIZZA" sign in neon. While she is talking, the
sign lights up for the evening.

                         NANCY
                     (on the phone)
I'm sorry. She'd already ordered it, and I couldn't get out of it.
                   (turning to the camera)
I'll be over as soon as I can.
                         (beat)
I love you, too. Ciao.

Nancy hangs up the phone and smiles wickedly, touching her tongue to her
teeth.

INT. JUNE AND NANCY'S KITCHEN

June has helped the Amazon into the house and gotten her into a chair. The
Amazon still seems dazed from the fall. The TV in the living room CONTINUES.

                          JUNE
Is there anything I can get you? A cup of tea?

                         AMAZON
No. Thank you.

                          JUNE
I could drive you over to the hospital. Are you sure you don't want
to -- ?

Julia Willis

                              AMAZON
No -- I'll be all right.

                               JUNE
                        (puzzling over it)
I just don't see how you could've -- I feel sort of responsible, I
guess.
                             (beat)
Do you live around here?

The Amazon, even in her disoriented state, realizes she'll have to come up with
some answers.

                              AMAZON
                            (thinking)
Uh -- no.

                               JUNE
Oh. Visiting?

                              AMAZON
Yes. I'm visiting.

                               JUNE
                  (trying to place the Amazon's style)
Where are you from? New York? San Francisco?

                              AMAZON
                            (quickly)
Yes.

                               JUNE
Which?

                              AMAZON
                    (indicating the living room)
What's that noise?

                               JUNE
Oh -- the TV? Does it bother you? I'll turn it off.

June goes into the living room. The Amazon looks around.

The CAMERA FOLLOWS the Amazon as she stands up shakily, takes a few
steps over to the refrigerator, starts to open it and sees a "DANGER! CALORIES!
KEEP OUT!" sign magnet on it. She takes her hand off the handle quickly and
wanders over to the sink.

She stares at the soapy water, tastes it with a finger and makes a face, and
inspects a bottle of "Dawn" detergent and a box of "Brillo" pads. She's turning
on the cold water faucet as June comes back.

JUNE'S P.O.V. - FROM THE DOOR
June sees the Amazon at the sink.

                    JUNE
       Are you thirsty?

The Amazon splashes the water in her face.

                    AMAZON
       No.

BACK TO SCENE

June comes over and hands her a dishtowel.

                    JUNE
       Here.

The Amazon takes the dishtowel, puts it in the sink, and wipes her face on her
sleeve.

                    JUNE
                 (continuing)
       Maybe you better sit down.

The Amazon sits down and June turns off the cold water.

                    JUNE
       I'm June -- Foster. Can you tell me your name?

                    AMAZON
       Yes . . . it's Dawn.

                    JUNE
       Dawn.

                    AMAZON
       Brillo.

                    JUNE
       Dawn Brillo?

                    AMAZON
       Dawn Brillo.

                    JUNE
       Okay. Um -- well, Dawn, would you like to lie down?

                    AMAZON
                 (innocently)
       With you?

June is a little shocked, but she laughs, taking it as a joke. (It doesn't hurt that
she finds the Amazon very attractive.)

                    JUNE
       No -- hardly. My -- my lover's on her way home with a pizza.

                    AMAZON
       Oh.

                              JUNE
Um -- that's interesting, that you automatically assume I'm a lesbian.

                             AMAZON
                            (shrugging)
Isn't everybody?

June laughs uncertainly. Then they HEAR the front door open, and she jumps
guiltily.

                              JUNE
That must be her now. Nan-cy?

                          NANCY (O.S.)
What-ey?

                              JUNE
                          (preparing her)
We have company.

Nancy enters the kitchen with the pizza box in her arms.

                             NANCY
I hope they like cold pizza.
                         (seeing a stranger)
Oh. Hello.

                             AMAZON
Hello.

                              JUNE
This is Dawn.
Nancy puts down the pizza box and gets plates from the cupboard.

                             NANCY
Do you know June from work?

                             AMAZON
No.

                              JUNE
Dawn had a bad fall out back. I brought her in.

                             NANCY
                         (always the lawyer)
On our property?

                              JUNE
On the edge -- in the alley.

                             NANCY
                           (concerned)
Are you all right? How did you fall?

                             AMAZON
I leaned out too far.

Amazon X   107

NANCY
What?

Nancy sits down at the table. June is at the refrigerator. The Amazon watches her ignore the "DANGER!" sign and open the door and take out a jug with no ill effects.

AMAZON
(mumbling)
Oh -- joke.

JUNE
(hearing the Amazon)
She's a little dazed. I think she might've hit her head.
(holding up the jug)
Apple juice all right?

NANCY
Don't we have any beer?

JUNE
(apologetic)
I forgot.

NANCY
(annoyed)
Fine, juice is fine.
(to the Amazon)
So how are you feeling?

AMAZON
All right -- a little dizzy.

NANCY
That could be a concussion. Do you have a doctor?

JUNE
She's not from around here, she's visiting.

AMAZON
From New York - San Francisco.

NANCY
New York *and* San Francisco?

AMAZON
Yes.

June gives them all glasses of juice.

JUNE
(to the Amazon)
Do you feel like eating?

AMAZON
Uh-huh.

Julia Willis

June puts a piece of pizza on her plate. The Amazon stares at it.

NANCY
New York *and* **San Francisco. You must do a lot of flying.**

AMAZON
Yes. I fly a lot.

She picks up the pizza with her hand, imitating June and Nancy, and takes a tiny bite. Nancy gives June an irritated look.

EXT. AN ALLEY BEHIND A ROW OF STORES - DUSK

A dumpster truck empties the dumpster and drops it with a loud CRASH. As it drives away, the Escapee appears from behind the loading dock -- she had enough warning to get out of the dumpster in time, but it was a close call. She and her clothes are dirtier than before. She runs off down the alley.

INT. LIZ'S APARTMENT - THE BEDROOM

Soft "New Age" MUSIC is PLAYING. The room is lit by candlelight -- there are at least two dozen candles placed all around, on every available surface. On the dresser there's a bottle of champagne cooling in a silver ice bucket and a bud vase holding one perfect rose.

(The intention here is to be terribly romantic but the effect is overdone, and there's something very impersonal about the room -- no photographs, no cosmetics, no clothes or books lying around -- it's like a stage set.)

LIZ enters, eating salad out of a bowl, wearing a lovely silk dressing gown. She is as perfect and impersonal as the room. She walks around, adjusting the candles, setting the stage, being a parody of "The Other Woman."

The PHONE RINGS, and she answers it seductively as she lies down on the bed.

LIZ
(on the phone)
Yes?

It's not Nancy, her secret love -- it's only her mother. She goes from being the ultimate temptress to a whining, sulky brat in two seconds flat.

LIZ
(continuing; impatient)
What, Ma? I can't, I'm busy, call Joey.
(beat)
Well, I'm going out, too, you just caught me ... a meeting. No, I can't, Ma. What kind of emergency?
(beat)
Ma, moving the couch is not an emergency ... no, not even if the "TV Guide" fell behind it, I'm sorry ...
(beat)
So change the channels and see for yourself. Ma ... you're bored, Ma, get a hobby -- I gotta go, no, I gotta go, I'll call you tomorrow.

She hangs up the phone and transforms herself back into a slinky, desirable woman. She picks up her salad bowl, and with her fingers takes a piece of lettuce and tears it with her teeth.

INT. JUNE AND NANCY'S LIVING ROOM

June follows Nancy out of the kitchen. Nancy is talking as she puts on her jacket to leave.

                    NANCY
I'll probably be late.
               (referring to the Amazon)
I think you should take her to the emergency room.

                    JUNE
She doesn't want to go – I already asked her.

                    NANCY
Well then, take her back to where she's staying. Just do something. She ought to be checked out – she's acting funny.

                    JUNE
I think she's sweet.

                    NANCY
You would. Don't you realize she could sue the pants off us, falling on our property?

                    JUNE
Oh, she wouldn't do that.

                    NANCY
Well, we're covered for falls. We're not covered for medical malpractice, so don't play doctor.
               (realizing the sexual implication)
You know what I mean – no herbal remedies.

Nancy is going out the door when June calls to her.

                    JUNE
Hey! Your briefcase.

Nancy, on her way to her erotic rendezvous, has forgotten she would take her briefcase to that advocates' meeting she is supposedly attending.

                    NANCY
Oh – right.

She crosses the room quickly and June gives her the briefcase, putting her hand on Nancy's arm. This makes Nancy uncomfortable.

                    JUNE
Nance – try not to be *too* late.

                    NANCY
I won't.

Julia Willis

                    JUNE
So we can plan for tomorrow.

                    NANCY
                  (blankly)
Tomorrow's Friday.

                    JUNE
Tomorrow's — oh, you didn't forget?

                    NANCY
Forget what?

                    JUNE
You mean you didn't take tomorrow off?

                    NANCY
No — why would I?

                    JUNE
                  (amazed)
Nancy, I told you three weeks ago I was taking a personal day
on the twenty-eighth and you said you'd take the day off, too —
so we could spend it together.

                    NANCY
Maybe I said I'd *try* to take the day off, but I never said for sure
I *would* — look, I can't help it if I'm busy.

                    JUNE
Nancy — we need to spend time together. We've got to talk.

                    NANCY
I know. We do ... we'll talk this weekend. Promise.

                    JUNE
                  (resigned)
Well — but what am I supposed to do about tomorrow? I expected
to have the whole day with you.

                    NANCY
Do something else — go to a movie — I don't know.

                    JUNE
Thanks. Thanks a lot.

                    NANCY
I'm sorry. I've got to go — bye.

She kisses June lightly again and goes out the door. June looks after her.
Is Nancy avoiding her? Could there be someone else?

EXT. NANCY'S PARKED CAR - NIGHT

Nancy reaches into the backseat, brings out flowers wrapped in tissue paper,
and puts them on the seat beside her.

                                             (CONTINUED)

CONTINUED:

Then she reaches under the seat, pulls out a bottle of champagne, and puts it beside the flowers. Finally, she pitches her briefcase in the backseat, starts her car, smiles in anticipation of the evening ahead, and drives away.

INT. JUNE AND NANCY'S KITCHEN

The Amazon is still sitting at the table, nibbling at her pizza and sniffing the pink flamingo salt shaker. June comes in.

JUNE

I just called Doris. She lives next door. She's a nurse.

The Amazon frowns and puts down the flamingo.

AMAZON

Nurse?

JUNE

She can just look you over and see that you're all right. And then I'll drive you home.

AMAZON

Home?

JUNE

Wherever you're staying. You know the address, don't you?

AMAZON
(looking around)

No.

JUNE

Oh ... well, what's the name?

AMAZON

Dawn Brillo.

JUNE

No – the name of the people you're staying with. Here in town.

AMAZON

Oh. June – June Foster.

JUNE

No, that's *my* name ...
(realizing what she means)
Oh.

The DOORBELL RINGS. It must be Doris. June finds it hard to take her eyes off the Amazon -- she seems almost hypnotized.

JUNE
(continuing)

I'll – I'll see who that is. Probably Doris.

Julia Willis

June goes to answer the front door. The Amazon picks up her own untouched glass of apple juice and sniffs it. It smells all right, so she drinks it down quickly. No sooner does she set the glass down than she becomes roaring drunk, giggling and weaving around the room.

> **AMAZON**
> Whee – Auntie Em, Toto, we're not in Kansas anymore.

She collapses in a heap on the floor.

EXT. THE SIDEWALK IN FRONT OF A GOODWILL STORE

Donations in boxes, piles, and garbage bags litter the sidewalk. Half a dozen women, poor and/or homeless, are picking through the clothes.

The Escapee comes warily around the corner, watches them for a minute, then tosses the sweater she was wearing and begins to pick through the clothes herself.

None of the other women acknowledge her presence until a BLACK WOMAN, middle-aged, with two little children huddled behind her, holds up a pullover sweater and, shining a flashlight on it, offers it to the Escapee.

> **BLACK WOMAN**
> Here, baby – you take this. It's your color.

The Escapee puts out her hand for the sweater. The other women go on about their business.

INT. JUNE AND NANCY'S LIVING ROOM

DORIS, a no-nonsense neighbor and nurse, a butch Thelma Ritter, is helping June carry the Amazon over to the couch. She is conscious but tipsy, with the weight and moveability of a sack of potatoes. They drop her on the couch, and she lands with a THUMP.

> **AMAZON**
> Whee!

> **JUNE**
> I don't understand this. Are you sure it's not a concussion?

Doris loosens the Amazon's collar, unfastens the object from the Amazon's wrist, and hands it to June.

> **DORIS**
> If it is, it's the first one I ever saw to come straight out of a bottle.

Doris goes back into the kitchen for her nurse's bag. June puts the object down on the coffee table and calls after her.

> **JUNE**
> But all she had was apple juice.

June looks down at the Amazon who smiles and waves at her. Doris comes back with her bag. She puts it down on a table, re-folding and repacking a stethoscope and blood pressure kit as she talks.

DORIS

What did she have before she fell over your trash can?

JUNE

I don't know exactly – but she wasn't drunk.

DORIS

You never know. Could be a binge – blackout – metabolism out of whack. Her pulse rate and blood pressure are a little low – reflexes okay – nothing unusual – no sign of concussion.

JUNE

So you don't think she should be in a hospital?

DORIS

If I were you, I'd get her into detox.
(seeing June's face)
Or just let her sleep it off – hope for the best.

On her way out, Doris pauses at the door.

DORIS
(continuing)

But if it was me, I'd call detox.

She leaves, and June stands looking down at the Amazon, who is giggling as she falls asleep. June watches her, mystified.

INT. LIZ'S LIVING ROOM

The living room is just as neatly sterile as her bedroom was. The DOORBELL RINGS, and Liz rushes from the bedroom to open the door. Nancy stands in the doorway, her arms full of flowers and champagne.

Liz sees her and starts to laugh; she apologizes for laughing while still giggling.

LIZ

I'm sorry, I'm really sorry – come in, come in.

Nancy enters, feeling self-conscious, and Liz leans against the door as she closes it.

LIZ
(continuing)

You aren't going to believe this, but I did the exact same thing.

Nancy doesn't understand and is rather embarrassed.

LIZ
(continuing; pointing)

Flowers – champagne? I got some, too. Isn't that funny?

NANCY
(getting it)

Oh ... well, you can never have too much of either.

                            LIZ
Absolutely not! Why don't we put yours on ice and start with
mine? ...
                        (suggestively)
It's in the bedroom.

                           NANCY
By all means.

Nancy hands Liz the bottle, and she takes it into a tiny kitchen.

INT. LIZ'S KITCHEN

With Nancy by her side, Liz puts Nancy's champagne in the refrigerator and
fills a vase with water for the flowers. Tired of waiting, Nancy puts the flowers
on the counter, steps up behind Liz, and puts her arms around Liz's waist.

Liz puts the vase on the counter, turns in Nancy's arms, and kisses her
passionately. They are aroused, as Liz breaks the clinch to put the flowers
in the vase.

                            LIZ
                            (coy)
I like your outfit – it's so professional.

                           NANCY
I didn't have time to change.

                            LIZ
No, it's yummy.

She finishes with the flowers and faces Nancy.

                            LIZ
                         (continuing)
It tells me you're dressed for success.

                           NANCY
So are you.

Liz smiles as Nancy steps toward her, pulling the sash free on her dressing
gown.

INT. JUNE AND NANCY'S BEDROOM

June is on the phone by the bed. We only hear her half of the conversation.

                           JUNE
                       (on the phone)
No, I guess I'll find out where she's staying and take her there.
Tonight ... or in the morning ... if she can remember. I certainly
can't put her out on the street ...

While she talks, she plays with the strange object Doris took off the Amazon's
wrist. June's back is to the dresser. As she absentmindedly clicks a button
on the object on and off, things on the dresser begin to levitate.

Amazon X   115

JUNE
(continuing)
God, Sal, I think I'm infatuated with this woman ... I feel like I'm dancing on air ...

June stops playing with the buttons and the things on the dresser stop moving.

JUNE
(continuing)
Ah, well – I better check on her again. So, can we have lunch tomorrow? One?
(beat)
Great. House of Hunan.
(another beat)
But Sal – you know, the funny thing is, I really don't *want* to take her home ...

INT. JUNE AND NANCY'S LIVING ROOM

The Amazon wakes up on the couch. As she sits up, her head is still fuzzy from the juice. She touches her wrist and misses the object she wears on it, sees the remote control on the coffee table, picks it up and presses several buttons.

THE AMAZON -- OVER THE SHOULDER -- TV

The TV comes on. A TELEVANGELIST COUPLE, dressed to the hilt in tacky, flashy clothes, is weeping openly into the camera.

WOMAN TELEVANGELIST
Bob, it just breaks my heart to think of those people out there who have no food, no place to sleep –

MAN TELEVANGELIST
Patty, we actually found a man huddled in a doorway and, if you can believe this, lying in his own excrement!

WOMAN TELEVANGELIST
(bawling)
Oh no!

MAN TELEVANGELIST
(in a trembling voice)
The odor of that man was simply overpowering.

WOMAN TELEVANGELIST
(taking her cue)
But Bob – what can we *do*?

MAN TELEVANGELIST
Patty, if everyone sitting at home would go to their phones right now and pledge $1000 to this ministry –

The Amazon presses a button and the channel is switched to a televised political discussion. There is a panel of several REPORTERS and a MODERATOR attempting to interview a pompous SENATOR who is objecting to their line of questioning.

> SENATOR
> — and I think it's important that we stick to the issues.

> REPORTER
> But Senator, isn't the key issue here your inability to understand the needs of these people, when you've never gone hungry a day in your life?

> SENATOR
> (serious)
> I have gone hungry on numerous occasions: on cook's night off, on the fairway nearing the eighteenth green — and once, circling O'Hare for two and a half hours, I had nothing but a roll of Lifesavers!
> (beat)
> Now — I want to get back to this defense budget.

The Amazon clicks to an interview program with two women, an INTERVIEWER and an AUTHOR.

CLOSEUP -- THE TV SCREEN

The Interviewer is introducing her guest.

> INTERVIEWER
> — and her new book, "How To Love An Unlovable Man." Lydia, welcome.

> AUTHOR
> Thank you, Penny.

> INTERVIEWER
> How did you come to write this book? Was there an unlovable man in your life?

> AUTHOR
> I think we all have unlovable men in our lives.

> INTERVIEWER
> (nodding)
> True, true.

> AUTHOR
> Men who don't touch, men who can't feel, men who have the emotional affect of a prune, men who when they hear the word "love" go catatonic —

> INTERVIEWER
> (interested)
> Uh-huh, uh-huh — and what can we do to help them?

                            AUTHOR
Penny, the key word Is patience.

                         INTERVIEWER
                        (nodding again)
Patience.

                            AUTHOR
Yes. It's also helpful to lower your expectations.

INT. LIZ'S BEDROOM

Most of the candles have burned down to little nubs in melted wax puddles. Nancy is lying in bed in a tangle of sheets. Two empty champagne glasses are on the bedside table, and the bottle is on the floor beside the bed.

Liz must be in the bathroom -- the TOILET FLUSHES. The CAMERA STAYS ON Nancy in bed as Liz comes back into the bedroom and pours more champagne.

                          LIZ (O.S.)
Now isn't this better than some old meeting?

                            NANCY
                      (groggy with pleasure)
What meeting?

Nancy moves over as Liz hops into bed beside her.

                             LIZ
Of course, you could call this a meeting, couldn't you? Of the minds . . .

Nancy moans softly. Liz passes her a champagne glass.

                            NANCY
                       (refusing gently)
I better not – I'm driving.

                             LIZ
                       (sipping it herself)
I'm not.
                            (beat)
Oh, wouldn't it be wonderful if you didn't have to go? If you could stay all night?

                            NANCY
That would be wonderful.

She kisses Liz, and they roll across the bed.

                             LIZ
So – when will this meeting be adjourned?

                            NANCY
Not until we've taken up every ounce of new business.

Liz squeals with delight, and they begin to make love again.

INT. JUNE AND NANCY'S LIVING ROOM - CLOSEUP - TV SCREEN

A commercial with a MOTHER and DAUGHTER. The Daughter is confessing her secret.

                    DAUGHTER
Mom, sometimes I – well, I just, down there – I smell, Mom.

                    MOTHER
                  (sympathetic)
Of course you do, dear. We all do – you, me, your grandmother.
Every woman does.

                    DAUGHTER
Then – it's all right?

                    MOTHER
                   (sincere)
Oh, no – it's *not* all right. It's just too real. And a man wants a
woman who's just as artificial as possible.

                    DAUGHTER
                  (frightened)
What can I do?

The Mother holds up a blowtorch with a label that says "FLAME FRESH."

                    MOTHER
Try what millions of women use every day to stay dry and odorfree.
                  (into the camera)
"FLAME FRESH."

TWO SHOT - JUNE AND THE AMAZON

June and the Amazon are sitting on the couch. June uses the remote control
to LOWER THE SOUND. The video continues, as hands demonstrate the
flame's effect on a wadded-up piece of paper.

                    JUNE
I hate this commercial.

She looks at the Amazon, who is still watching the screen intently. It is obvious
that June is very taken with the Amazon.

On the TV the Mother and Daughter are going down the beach together,
hand in hand, walking with their legs spread wide apart (the result of using
"FLAME FRESH"). The Daughter swings the blowtorch in her other hand.
The Amazon turns to June.

                    AMAZON
This is a very strange planet.

                    JUNE
You don't watch much television, do you?

AMAZON
(proudly)
I've seen "The Wizard Of Oz." Many times.

June begins babbling like a teenager on a first date.

JUNE
Isn't that great how they show it every year? And now you can get it on video – we've got a VCR, but we never seem to have the time to rent the movies – and a lot of these new movies I wouldn't watch – but "The Wizard Of Oz," it's such a classic . . . Because we all want to go over the rainbow, I guess.
(a slight chuckle)
I wouldn't have minded going over it today.

AMAZON
Why?

JUNE
Oh, I don't know – burnout at work, meltdown at home –
(changes the subject)
Oh, and I forgot – Doris took this off your wrist while you were – sleeping. What is it, anyway, some sort of beeper-calculator-micro-word-processor – ?

June hands the Amazon the object, which is actually her wrist transmitter. The Amazon puts it back on.

AMAZON
Just something to help me – whenever I go over the rainbow.

The Amazon smiles and June laughs, taking it as a joke.

JUNE
Can I get you anything? Some apple juice?

AMAZON
(positive)
No – no juice.

JUNE
(casual)
Dawn, do you want me to take you somewhere – or would you like to stay here tonight?

AMAZON
I'd like to stay here.

JUNE
(relieved)
Good. That would be nice.

AMAZON
(indicating the bedroom)
Shall I stay with you? In there?

　　　　　　　　　　　　　　　　　　Julia Willis

                              JUNE
            No -- you'd better stay out here.

The Amazon begins to unbutton her spacesuit.

                             AMAZON
           All right. You and Nancy have an agreement, don't you?

                              JUNE
           Yes.

                             AMAZON
           I understand.

The Amazon slips out of the sleeves of her spacesuit. She is naked
underneath. Her movements are so easy and graceful, so completely unself-
conscious, that June can hardly bear to watch her.

                              JUNE
           I'll -- get you a blanket and pillow.

June goes out. The Amazon slips off the rest of her spacesuit and folds it
neatly. On the TV screen is a mugshot of the Escapee. When the Amazon
sees it, she grabs the remote control and BRINGS UP THE VOLUME.

CLOSEUP - THE TV SCREEN

The late news is reporting on the Escapee story. There is a PANNING SHOT
of the back of the courthouse.

                        ANCHORPERSON (V.O.)
           -- escaped through a side door, wearing prison coveralls and a pink
           sweater taken from a cleaning woman she encountered on a service
           elevator.

SHOTS of the neighborhood and the house the Escapee lived in with her
husband.

                        ANCHORPERSON (V.O.)
                           (continuing)
           Meanwhile, Dennis Bradley remains in satisfactory condition at Mass
           General, and those neighbors who yesterday were shocked by the
           incident seem to think today it's back to business as usual.

An elderly NEIGHBOR LADY is interviewed. Another lady beside her nods,
and a few kids on bicycles behind her wave at the camera. A VOICE O.S.
asks a question.

                           VOICE (O.S.)
           Are you afraid she might be hiding out in this neighborhood?

                         NEIGHBOR LADY
           Oh, no -- why would she come back here when he never let her out
           of the house? She's long gone by now -- halfway to the moon.

THE AMAZON - OVER THE SHOULDER - TV

As the Amazon LOWERS the volume, the TV picture goes back to the anchor desk. The Anchorperson is still talking, and the mugshot of the Escapee is an inset in the upper right hand corner of the screen.

CLOSE SHOT - THE AMAZON

The Amazon stares hard at the Escapee's picture and touches her own face.

MATCH CUT T0:

EXT. A LONELY STREET NEAR AN ABANDONED BUILDING - CLOSE SHOT - THE FACE OF THE ESCAPEE

The Escapee walks along, looking for a place to hide for the night. THE CAMERA PULLS BACK TO REVEAL she is dressed in Goodwill clothes, with a wool cap pulled down on her head. Now she's not the woman the police are searching for -- she's just another street woman.

INT. JUNE AND NANCY'S BEDROOM

June is in bed alone, rehearsing what she'll say to the Amazon in the morning.

> JUNE
> (bright and cheerful)
> Good morning -- would you like some breakfast?
> (tries again)
> Good morning -- did you sleep well?
> (a third time)
> Good morning -- my, you have a nice body.

She pictures the Amazon's nice body and sighs. Then she HEARS Nancy unlocking the front door, snaps off the bedside light, and pretends to be asleep.

INT. JUNE AND NANCY'S LIVING ROOM

The Amazon lies on the couch. She is covered by a blanket, has her feet (with spaceboots still on) up on the pillow, and is using a towel on top of her folded spacesuit for a headrest. A washcloth sits on top of her head. The lights are on and her eyes are wide open.

Nancy comes in the door. At first she doesn't see the Amazon. Humming "OVER THE RAINBOW," she crosses to her desk and puts down her briefcase.

> AMAZON
> (quietly)

Hello.

> NANCY
> (startled)

Oh!

> (coming over)

So -- you're still with us.

Her afterglow of passion has been replaced by exhaustion. She is not especially pleased to see the Amazon.

                            AMAZON
        I'm feeling much better.

                            NANCY
        Good . . . aren't your friends, the ones you're staying with, aren't
        they worried about you?

                            AMAZON
        I'm staying here. June asked me.

                            NANCY
        Oh.
                            (sarcastic)
        You always wear a washcloth to bed?

                            AMAZON
        No.

She takes the washcloth off her head, sniffing the air and looking up at Nancy. Nancy, leaving, gives her a little wave.

                            NANCY
        Good night.

                            AMAZON
                            (frowning)
        I thought you and June had an agreement.

                            NANCY
        Huh?

                            AMAZON
                            (sniffing again)
        You've been with someone else.

                            NANCY
        What?

                            AMAZON
        With someone else -- I can smell it.

Nancy starts to sniff her own clothes and then stops.

                            NANCY
        Don't be absurd.

                            AMAZON
        You washed, but it's still there. The smell of another woman.

                            NANCY
                            (angrily)
        Listen -- you shut up!
                            (lying)
        I've done nothing of the kind . . . and don't you go saying that to
        June.

Amazon X   123

                              AMAZON
I won't tell her. *You* must tell her.

                              NANCY
I'm not telling her anything.
                         (backing away)
You're crazy -- and I want you out of here in the morning.

ANGLE ON THE AMAZON

The Amazon watches Nancy go. Thoughtfully, she places the washcloth on top of her head again.

INT. JUNE AND NANCY'S BEDROOM

Nancy enters, feeling a little unnerved.

                              NANCY
    June? Junie? Honey?

June doesn't answer. We SEE that she is lying on her side, her eyes open, feeling guilty about her feelings for the Amazon. In the b.g. Nancy pauses at the dresser, picks up a bottle, sprays herself with hairspray and coughs. June frowns -- what's that about?

INT. HALLWAY OF AN ABANDONED BUILDING

The Escapee comes hesitantly into the half-dark hallway, a garbage bag in one hand, her gun in the other. There are several motionless bundles huddled along the walls. ONE OF THE BUNDLES stirs and speaks -- a woman's voice.

                           BUNDLE #1
    Who the fuck are you?
The Escapee takes a step back.

                            ESCAPEE
                        (almost shouting)
    I have a gun.

                           BUNDLE #1
    So shoot me -- I got nothing to lose.

A SECOND BUNDLE speaks. It's another woman.

                           BUNDLE #2
    Ah, lay down and go to sleep.

Both bundles curl up and are quiet. The Escapee crouches down and makes a pillow of her garbage bag. Tucking the gun inside her jacket, she cautiously closes her eyes and tries to sleep.

                                              DISSOLVE TO:

EXT. JUNE AND NANCY'S HOUSE - MORNING - ESTABLISHING

A bright, sunny day: BIRDS SINGING, an ALARM CLOCK BUZZING, followed by a RADIO BLASTING. The MORNING NEWSCASTER is speaking, with the TELETYPE UNDER.

                    MORNING NEWSCASTER (V.O.)
          -- remains at large this morning. It is now presumed she may have
          left the area. A woman fitting her description was reportedly
          sighted, along with a male companion --

INT. JUNE AND NANCY'S BEDROOM

June is in bed, her pillow over her head. Nancy's side of the bed has been slept in, but she is already up. As the RADIO CLOCK BLARES on, one of June's arms flails at the clock but can't reach it.

                    MORNING NEWSCASTER (V.O.)
                         (continuing)
          -- in the parking lot of a Motel 6 in Burlington, Vermont. Meanwhile,
          her husband, who alleges she shot him three times with his own
          gun, is resting comfortably at a local hospital.

The TELETYPE changes to a HELICOPTER WHIR. JACKIE JAMES is the friendly traffic reporter.

                    MORNING NEWSCASTER (V.O.)
                         (continuing)
          And now we go to Jackie James for this traffic update.

                    JACKIE (V.O.)
                         (cheerful and upbeat)
          Thanks, Jim. That overturned tractor-trailer full of pistachio nuts
          near the Allston-Brighton tollbooth has closed the turnpike to all
          incoming traffic, and your best bet'll be --

Nancy CLICKS OFF the RADIO.

                    NANCY
          -- to stay home.

June pulls the pillow off her head.

                    JUNE
                         (sleepily)
          Thank you.

Nancy is already dressed, and is putting on her shoes, watch, etc., and brushing her hair.

                    NANCY
          Did you hear any of that?

                    JUNE
          I never use the turnpike.

NANCY

No -- the thing about that woman who escaped.

JUNE

Vaguely.

NANCY

Did it not cross your mind that the mysterious stranger bedded down on our couch might *be* that woman?

Reminded of the Amazon, June comes wide awake.

JUNE

What? No . . .

NANCY
(interrogating the witness)

Do you know who she is?

JUNE
(defensively)

Dawn Brillo.

NANCY

Sounds like a bad alias. Do you know where she comes from?

JUNE

I know she was hurt and she needed attention.

NANCY
(a little dig)

Which you were more than happy to provide.

JUNE
(digging back)

Well, it sure beats sitting home alone all night.

Nancy backs off, but as she gets ready to leave she gives June one last warning.

NANCY

Aiding and abetting an escaped criminal is serious business, June -- you better get rid of her, and fast.

JUNE
(shocked by her coldness)

I don't think I know you anymore.

NANCY

Maybe you don't.

She walks out of the room, leaving June surprised and hurt.

EXT. JUNE AND NANCY'S BACKYARD - MED. SHOT - THE AMAZON

The Amazon is awake and dressed, standing by the same spot where she fell the night before. Using the transmitter on her wrist, as well as her own mental powers, she is communicating with her ship.

> **AMAZON (V.O.)**
> -- and I will need another twenty-four hours to study the situation further and take appropriate action.

She is answered by a woman's SPACE VOICE in her head.

> **SPACE VOICE (O.S.)**
> Be careful down there -- lions and tigers and bears.

> **AMAZON (V.O.)**
> Oh my.
> (signing off)
> Love.

> **SPACE VOICE (O.S.)**
> Love.

The Amazon takes a deep breath and closes her eyes, trying to visualize the location of Linda Bradley, the Escapee.

> **AMAZON**
> (chanting aloud)
> There's no place like home -- Linda Bradley -- there's no place like home.

INT. THE HALLWAY OF AN ABANDONED BUILDING

Light streams in through the doorway and various cracks, but the hallway is still dark and gloomy.

The Escapee awakens and grabs her gun. Loud talking has startled her. Several of the bundles from the night before have moved on. Bundle #1 is curled up on the floor and Bundle #2 is standing over her, shouting as if Bundle #1 were deaf.

> **BUNDLE #2**
> I thought you were dead!

> **BUNDLE #1**
> So what?

> **BUNDLE #2**
> Ain't you getting up? The van's coming.

> **BUNDLE #1**
> (waving her away)
> Go on -- I'll be there later.

> **BUNDLE #2**
> (shuffling off)
> Okay -- long as you ain't dead.

Bundle #2 passes the wide-eyed Escapee nervously and goes out. The Escapee rubs the sleep out of her eyes and sits up on her haunches, the gun in her hand. She looks over at Bundle #1, MARY, who is now sitting up. Mary's an old woman who's seen it all.

> MARY
> Jesus, kid, what do you think this is, the Old West or sumpin'?

INT. JUNE AND NANCY'S KITCHEN

Nancy is at the kitchen table, drinking a cup of coffee and finishing a microwave breakfast, when the Amazon bounces through the back door. She spills her coffee.

> NANCY
> Oh, for -- you scared me to death.

> AMAZON
> (studying her)
> No, I didn't. I would say you're very much alive.

> NANCY
> Uh-huh. So -- called anyone to come and get you yet?

> AMAZON
> (using Nancy's tone)
> No -- have you told June Foster about your lover yet?

Nancy has had enough breakfast and quite enough of the Amazon. She stands up and heads for the door.

> NANCY
> If you're here when I get home tonight, I'm calling the police. And I think you know why!

She storms out, leaving the Amazon puzzled. The Amazon sticks a finger in Nancy's leftover coffee and licks it as the front DOOR SLAMS.

Again, she has an adverse reaction -- but she barely tasted it, so she doesn't pass out. She quickly looks in the kitchen cabinets for an antidote. She opens the freezer, sees more microwave boxes, grabs a tray of ice, rushes it to the sink and dumps it.

Taking a handful of ice cubes, she rubs them over her face and behind her neck. The ice brings her around just as June comes into the kitchen. June is still hurt by Nancy's attitude but *so* infatuated with the Amazon. Her opening line sounds rehearsed. It was.

> JUNE
> Good morning!

The Amazon turns around, refreshed, her hands full of ice.

> AMAZON
> Aah . . . hello.

> JUNE
> I guess that'll wake you up.

AMAZON

It helps.

June gets a cup and pours herself some coffee. The Amazon drops the ice in the sink.

JUNE

In Sweden they rub their faces with snow in the morning. Or maybe that was just Garbo in a movie . . . have you had coffee?

AMAZON

Yes, plenty.

JUNE
(seeing Nancy's leftovers)

But you haven't eaten?

AMAZON

No.

JUNE

I'm not a morning person.
(sipping her coffee)
I wonder if you could start us some breakfast while I shower -- think so?

AMAZON

Sure.

As June starts out with her coffee, she remembers how dazed and tipsy the Amazon was the night before.

JUNE

You're feeling better now, aren't you? Better than last night, I mean.

AMAZON

Yes, I feel fine now.

JUNE

Yes -- you look good.

AMAZON
(pleasantly)

You look good, too.

June gives a little laugh and backs shyly out the door.

INT. BALLOON STORE

Nancy is ordering balloons for Liz, writing down the address.

NANCY

Can you make them all purple?

The SALESGIRL is a young lesbian. She smiles.

SALESGIRL

You mean lavender?

                    NANCY
Yes -- lavender.

                    SALESGIRL
I think that can be arranged.

                    NANCY
Good. Let's see -- it'll have to be after six o'clock -- she gets off
at five . . . well, make it six-thirty. No -- seven.

                    SALESGIRL
                 (writing it down)
Seven.

The Salesgirl gives Nancy back her credit card and thanks her. Nancy thinks
of one more thing.

                    NANCY
Oh -- and do you charge extra for singing?

INT. JUNE AND NANCY'S BATHROOM

June dries off after her shower and puts her robe on, singing "Over the
Rainbow" all the while. She has a little trouble with the high notes.

                    JUNE
"Where da-da-da like da-da drops --"

She sees the old message, "WE NEED TO TALK!," on the bathroom mirror.
Impulsively, she grabs a hand towel and wipes it off.

                    JUNE
"DA-da-da-da-da-chimneytops --"

She throws down the towel and flings open the bathroom door.

                    JUNE
"DA-DA-DA-DA-DA-ME!"

INT. JUNE AND NANCY'S KITCHEN

The Amazon has something in the microwave. She watches it carefully,
coaxing it aloud.

                    AMAZON
Come on now -- you can do it.

The microwave BELL RINGS and there's a KNOCK at the back door. She
goes from one to the other, decides on the door and opens it. There's a
METER READER in uniform on the steps.

                    METER READER
                    (bored)
Gas.

Julia Willis

                              AMAZON
                      (responding carefully)
        Oh. Uh -- no thanks -- I don't drive.

She closes the door and goes back to the microwave. Another KNOCK at
the door. June, dressed, comes in and goes quickly to the door.

                               JUNE
        I'll get that.

She opens the door as the Amazon takes the food out of the microwave and
puts it on the table.

                          METER READER
                          (still bored)
        Gas.

                               JUNE
                            (pointing)
        Around the side.

June closes the door.

The Amazon misses that exchange -- she is standing proudly by the table
where she has placed the microwave trays. She remembers forks, gets two
out of the sink drainer and places them beside the trays.

                              AMAZON
        There. There.

Meanwhile, June sits down and stares first at her tray, then at the Amazon's.
She picks up her fork and pokes at the food.

                               JUNE
        Oh. Veal scallopini.

The Amazon sits down, picks up her fork, and takes a bite. It's good -- so
why isn't June eating?

                              AMAZON
        Something wrong?

                               JUNE
                        (puts down her fork)
        I'm not a big breakfast eater.

The Amazon realizes this is not what June eats for breakfast. She puts
down her fork, too.

                              AMAZON
        This isn't right, is it? This isn't breakfast.

                               JUNE
        It's -- *unusual* for breakfast.

The Amazon decides to tell June the truth.

                    AMAZON
June Foster?

                    JUNE
Call me June.

                    AMAZON
June.

                    JUNE
Dawn.

                    AMAZON
I'm not Dawn . . . I'm not who I said I was.

                    JUNE
Oh.

June thinks the Amazon is admitting she's the Escapee.

                    AMAZON
                    (confessing)
**I've never told a lie before -- it's an awful feeling ... I haven't been
telling you the truth about myself. I'm not from New York-San
Francisco.**

                    JUNE
I see.

                    AMAZON
**You've been so nice, and it's only fair that I tell you the truth . . .
I just hope I'm doing the right thing, and you won't tell anyone
else.**

Prepared for the worst, June places her hand over the Amazon's.

                    AMAZON
                    (continuing)
You see, I really shouldn't be here at all. It was an accident.

                    JUNE
                    (nodding)
You mean you're innocent.

                    AMAZON
Oh, no -- it was my fault -- I shouldn't have leaned out so far.

                    JUNE
Huh?

                    AMAZON
**I leaned out too far -- when I was examining your garbage -- and I
fell.**

                    JUNE
My garbage?

Julia Willis

AMAZON
I know, I know, it was stupid – but I just got excited. This is only my second trip to Earth.

June gently eases her hand back.

JUNE
Really ...

AMAZON
Yes. I'm a gatherer from another universe – I'm here studying Earth culture.

JUNE
(blankly)
Uh-huh ...

AMAZON
You don't believe me ... well, I can understand that. You live in a world of great skepticism. It's always possible to lie here – in my world it is not.

JUNE
But if you're not Dawn, you've already lied.

AMAZON
Only because my real name is rather – unusual. And it's easy to lie here. Oh, but June, it wasn't easy lying to you.

JUNE
That's what they all say.

AMAZON
All right, I must prove myself to you ...
(beat)
I can tell you anything about your life.

JUNE
How? By reading my garbage?

AMAZON
No – private things, things no one else knows. Ask me, please.

JUNE
(curious)
Something no one ... okay – how many orgasms have I had this month?

The Amazon fiddles with her wrist transmitter and touches her forehead with her fingertips.

AMAZON
(referring to the transmitter)
I could do without this at home, but here thought waves are so jumbled –
(beat; then the answer)
None.

June is not a believer yet.

JUNE
Yeah, well – Nancy could've told you that – I don't know *why*, but . . .

AMAZON
No – Nancy thinks you've had two. You faked them.

JUNE
(amazed)
How could you – ?

AMAZON
I guess that's too personal – how about a little magic trick?

The Amazon turns a dial on the transmitter and the flamingo salt and pepper shakers dance in the air.

AMAZON
(continuing; her eyes on the flamingos)
You're a very lovely woman, June Foster. You deserve more orgasms.

JUNE
(in shock; also watching the flamingos)
Turn that thing off before I have one.

EXT. OUTSIDE THE ABANDONED BUILDING

The Escapee is with Mary, who is trying to get her to go along to the van that gives out free coffee and donuts to the homeless.

BUNDLE #1
The coffee stinks, but the donuts are all right.

ESCAPEE
I don't think so.

MARY
Jelly – they got coconut, they got Bavarian cream –

ESCAPEE
Look – is there a place around here I could hop a freight without being seen?

MARY
(tilting her head)
Say – you must be hot. What'd you do, kid?

ESCAPEE
Nothing. Never mind.

She starts to go off on her own.

MARY
Hey – wait a minute. I don't care. Nobody cares down here . . .
(going for donuts)
Come on, before they run out of my favorites.

I have to get out of here.

                    MARY

Don't you get it, kid? Pull your cap down, drag that bag – you're home free. You don't exist no more – you're invisible, see? The cops won't even notice you unless you been dead two-three days.
                  (shuffling off)
Come on – trust me, you're in the clear. Come have a donut with Mary.

The Escapee watches Mary shuffling away for a moment, then runs to catch up with her.

INT. DONUT SHOP

The Amazon and June are sitting at the counter, having coffee and donuts.

CLOSE SHOT - THE AMAZON

The Amazon picks up her donut and looks through the hole.

                    AMAZON

Interesting.

BACK TO SCENE

June treats the Amazon as if she were breakable -- she's rather in awe of the alien.

                    JUNE

It's sugar-glazed.

                    AMAZON

I was referring to the shape.

                    JUNE

Oh.

                    AMAZON
                (taking a little bite)

Very like my ship.

                    JUNE

How – how can your ship be in our backyard without anyone seeing it?

                    AMAZON

Oh, the ship never comes in this close – I was in a collection tank.
                  (using her hands)
Like a big bucket ... but you wouldn't see it *or* the ship.

                    JUNE

Why not?

Amazon X   135

AMAZON

We're really operating from another dimension – no one ever sees us ... they say that some years ago we could be sensed by people taking LSD – but no more.
(speaking like a hippie)
There's like no good acid around anymore, man.

JUNE

But if no one can see you, how is it you're *here* – how do *I* see you?

AMAZON

(referring to the wrist transmitter)
This is programmed to project me into your world in case of an accident – so I won't get lost in between ... or stepped on if I should fall. So here I am.

JUNE

You certainly are. But shouldn't we be going down to the United Nations, or the White House or something? Don't you want to make a speech?

The Amazon laughs.

AMAZON

I hate speeches – they put me to sleep. That's not my department, June. I just look at the way things are on your planet.

JUNE

Not much like life where you're from, I guess.

AMAZON

No – but remarkably comparable to the way things were on my planet several hundred thousand years ago, when there was war and crime and greed and pollution – before the men exterminated themselves.
(enthusiastic)
And all of that is here now – this is a living, breathing, terribly primitive environment.

JUNE

(embarrassed)
Yeah – we're real proud of that. So ... what would you like to do?

AMAZON

I'd like to spend your day with you – just a typical day.

JUNE

I'm afraid I'll bore you to tears.

AMAZON

The trouble with you, June Foster – you've forgotten how very beautiful you are.

She takes June's hand.

Julia Willis

AMAZON
(continuing)
I think you're fascinating.

Flustered, June takes her hand back and puts two dollar bills on the counter.

JUNE
Don't you want your coffee?

AMAZON
It doesn't agree with me.

The Amazon weaves on her stool to demonstrate. She has already explained to June about the apple juice.

JUNE
Oh . . .

They get up together. The Amazon has the rest of her donut in her hand, as the WAITRESS comes over and picks up the money. The Amazon points to the donut.

AMAZON
(to the Waitress)
This is very good. Especially the part in the middle.

She follows June out. The Waitress clears their places.

WAITRESS
(monotone)
Ha-ha.

EXT. THE SIDEWALK BESIDE THE COFFEE VAN

Mary and the Escapee are getting coffee and donuts out of the back of a van parked on the street. A HOMELESS COUNSELOR is serving them. The Escapee has her wool cap pulled way down over her face.

HOMELESS COUNSELOR
Sorry, Mary — that's all I got left.

MARY
No chocolate?

HOMELESS COUNSELOR
Just the plain. You almost missed me — I was about to pack up and go.
(to the Escapee)
You're new, aren't you?

The Escapee takes her cup and donut and turns her back. Mary speaks for her, making up a story to excuse her behavior.

MARY
She ain't right in the head. She hears things. She sees Martians.

                    HOMELESS COUNSELOR
Sounds like that Lily Tomlin show.

                            MARY
Huh?

                    HOMELESS COUNSELOR
Oh, there's this character on the streets who talks to spacemen.

                            MARY
                    (taking her literally)
Yeah, it happens ... but she's okay. I look after her.

There are three donuts left in the box the Counselor is holding.

                    HOMELESS COUNSELOR
One more?

Mary takes the whole box. She gestures toward the Escapee.

                            MARY
She's a growing girl.

INT. NANCY'S OFFICE

Nancy is on the phone with Liz, playing with a fertility goddess paperweight
as she talks. Her back is to the door, so she doesn't see PHYLLIS entering
quietly. Phyllis is Nancy's law partner -- she's sharp, wisecracking, the Eve
Arden type.

                            NANCY
                    (on the phone)
Mmm ... I would love to go away with you ... soon ... I know ...
                            (beat)
Oh, and I hope you like surprises –

Nancy swivels her chair around and sees Phyllis. Without missing a beat,
she cuts the conversation short.

                            NANCY
                    (continuing)
Oops, I've got to run – I'll call you later. Bye.

Nancy hangs up the phone. Phyllis is curious.

                            PHYLLIS
She and Sal are having lunch today.

                            NANCY
                    (noncommittal)
Really?

                            PHYLLIS
She didn't mention it?

                            NANCY
No – no, she didn't.

                    PHYLLIS
I'm assuming that was June on the phone.

                    NANCY
                  (ignoring that)
Marcia said you had a question?

                    PHYLLIS
Could be I have several.

                    NANCY
I'm only taking business questions this morning.

                    PHYLLIS
But you're not just taking business calls.

Nancy puts the fertility goddess down on a stack of papers.

                    NANCY
When I'm ready to tell you, Phyl, I'll tell you. Meanwhile, drop it.

                    PHYLLIS
Okay, Counselor.
                  (beat)
But – I will say I'd be very sorry to see you and June break up.

                    NANCY
Not everybody is like you and Sal, you know. Not everybody can
be monogamous for a hundred years.

                    PHYLLIS
                  (deadpan)
A hundred and five.
                  (down to business)
I wanted to know whether you could have those Henderson
interrogatories ready by next week.

                    NANCY
Yes, I can.

Phyllis walks to the door and pauses with her hand on the doorknob.

                    PHYLLIS
Good.
                  (beat)
I'll knock next time.

                    NANCY
I will tell you, Phyl – soon.
                  (apologetic)
This has all been very sudden.

                    PHYLLIS
It always is, dear.

Phyllis leaves.

ANGLE ON NANCY

Now Nancy realizes the far-reaching consequences of her actions and has a brief moment of regret. Then she picks up the phone to call Liz back.

EXT. DOWNTOWN INTERSECTION - JUNE'S MOVING CAR

June and the Amazon are in June's car. June is driving. They cross an intersection and the CAMERA PANS to

MARY AND THE ESCAPEE

who are walking on the cross street. The Escapee follows June's car with her eyes, a startled expression on her face. She couldn't have actually seen the Amazon, but she felt something -- an affinity. Mary is talking.

>   MARY
> I do okay on Tremont – but they got more of a criminal element.
> You oughta come with me – protect an old lady.
>   (no response)
> Whatsa matter, too proud to do a little panhandling?

She stops and looks up at the Escapee, who is still staring in the direction of June's car.

>   MARY
>   (continuing)
> Say – what gives? You look like you seen a ghost ... huh?

>   ESCAPEE
>   (bewildered)
> I – don't know.

>   MARY
> You don't look so good, kid. Maybe you been talking to them spacemen, huh?
>   (reaching into her bag)
> Here – have a donut.

The Escapee takes the donut Mary offers and stares at it. Somehow the shape of the donut seems familiar (the shape of the Amazon's ship, though she doesn't know that).

CLOSEUP - DONUT

The Escapee looks through the hole with one eye.

MATCH DISSOLVE TO:

INT. THE PLAYROOM AT JUNE'S WORKPLACE - CLOSEUP - RING-TOSS

We are LOOKING AT a rubber ring-toss with the Amazon's eye staring through the hole in the middle.

Julia Willis

THE PLAYROOM - FULL SHOT

REVEALS she is standing in the playroom corner of a waiting room in a community mental health/social services place that was originally a private residence. There are child abuse, AIDS, and ALA-TEEN posters on the walls.

The Homeless Counselor (who earlier was serving coffee and donuts to Mary and the Escapee) comes down the hall past the waiting room and notices the Amazon.

                    HOMELESS COUNSELOR
        Is someone helping you?

                    AMAZON
        I'm waiting for June Foster. We're here to pick up her check.

                    HOMELESS COUNSELOR
        Oh.

The Counselor stares at the Amazon. She is vaguely reminded of the Escapee but can't make the connection.

                    HOMELESS COUNSELOR
                    (continuing)
        Have we met?

The Amazon is shaking her head as June joins them.

                    JUNE
        Okay, let's – oh, hi, Ellen.
                    (a little nervous)
        Uh – this is my friend Dawn.

The Counselor puts out her hand and the Amazon shakes it; the Counselor notices the Amazon's wrist transmitter.

                    HOMELESS COUNSELOR
        Oh – I love your watch.

                    AMAZON
        Thank you.

June wants to get the Amazon out of there quickly.

                    JUNE
        Well, we've got to run before someone brings me a problem.

                    HOMELESS COUNSELOR
        I had a problem with the coffee van this morning.

The Amazon picks up a Slinky toy.

                    JUNE
        Oh?

                    HOMELESS COUNSELOR
        Brake fluid – leak – I dropped it off on my way back – should be ready this afternoon.

Amazon X   141

                              JUNE
Great – all taken care of.

                    HOMELESS COUNSELOR
                 (still staring at the Amazon)
Are you sure we haven't met? Do you play volleyball?

                           AMAZON
                   (playing with the Slinky)
No.

                    HOMELESS COUNSELOR
                    (racking her brain)
God, where have I seen you? At the park?

                              JUNE
She's just visiting, Ellen.

                           AMAZON
                       (still playing)
I'm visiting.

She wraps the Slinky around her neck. June smiles uncomfortably at the
Counselor.

EXT. THE FRONT ENTRANCE TO JUNE'S BANK - ESTABLISHING

June's car is parked on the street outside the bank.

INT. BANK

June and the Amazon are waiting in the bank line. June has been explaining
her work to the Amazon -- she speaks in a whisper and sounds tired just
talking about it.

                              JUNE
– and if my grant proposal's accepted, we'll have the money for
a twenty-bed facility for homeless women ... oh, I don't know, I
really love what I'm doing – I'm just burnt out.

The Amazon nods, glancing around the bank. She whispers back.

                           AMAZON
Why is it so quiet in here?

                              JUNE
Because it's a bank – serious stuff.

                           AMAZON
Like in a church?

                              JUNE
Yeah. We come here to pray over our money.

                           AMAZON
                     (taking her seriously)
Why?

                                    JUNE
So we won't lose it and end up in a twenty-bed facility.

                                   AMAZON
So people really need this money, don't they?

                                    JUNE
Yep — that's the system.

A TELLER calls out "Next, please" and June goes up to deposit her check. The Amazon looks at a sign on a stand that says "WE'RE HERE TO HELP!" ANOTHER TELLER calls out "NEXT, PLEASE" and the Amazon gets a shove from behind. She goes over to the Teller.

                              ANOTHER TELLER
May I help you?

                                   AMAZON
Yes — I'd like some money.

                              ANOTHER TELLER
Do you have an account with us?

                                   AMAZON
No — I'm just visiting.

                              ANOTHER TELLER
All right. If you wish to cash an out-of-town check, I'll need two photo I.D.s and two major credit cards.

                                   AMAZON
I don't have a check.

                              ANOTHER TELLER
Then what is it you want?

                                   AMAZON
I would like some money — for the twenty-bed facility.
                              (indicating the sign)
You're "here to help?"

                              ANOTHER TELLER
I'll get the manager.

                                                    QUICK CUT TO:

EXT. A TALL PHALLIC BUILDING UNDER CONSTRUCTION - LATE MORNING - LONG SHOT

As the CAMERA PANS from the top of the building down to the base (where a CONSTRUCTION WORKER, hardhat and all, is standing near the canteen truck), we can HEAR June and the Amazon as they are walking past the construction site.

                                 JUNE (O.S.)
From now on, ask me, okay? Banks have no sense of humor ...
and they don't give away their money, either.

AMAZON (O.S.)
Then why did the sign say they were here to help?

JUNE (O.S.)
That's just advertising.

The CAMERA ZOOMS in

ON THE SIDEWALK BY THE CANTEEN TRUCK

as the Amazon stops walking. June stops beside her. They are standing beside the canteen truck with the Construction Worker in the b.g. -- he is eating a Hostess Twinkie and leering at them.

AMAZON
Like commercials? Like what's on the cans and boxes and plastic wrappers?

JUNE
Exactly.

AMAZON
Oh.

The Construction Worker behind them makes a nasty kissing NOISE with his lips. He has Twinkie crumbs on his face.

JUNE
(annoyed)
Get lost.

She wants to walk on, but the Amazon is curious and goes directly over to him.

AMAZON
Excuse me – why did you make that noise?

CONSTRUCTION WORKER
(grinning)
What noise?

He takes another sloppy bite of his Twinkie. June calls to the Amazon.

JUNE
Dawn –

AMAZON
(to the Construction Worker)
I don't understand – why is it you hate me?

CONSTRUCTION WORKER
Huh?

AMAZON
(reading him like an ancient artifact)
Oh – it isn't just me. You hate all women.

CONSTRUCTION WORKER
Ah, you're crazy — I don't hate women.

AMAZON
Oh, yes — you do.

CONSTRUCTION WORKER
What're you, calling me a fag or something?

JUNE
Uh — Dawn —

AMAZON
(to June)
Yes — just a moment.
(back to him)
I know I shouldn't be interfering in your life this way, but it's really important that you recognize the basic humanity you share with women.

The Construction Worker reaches for the belt on his pants.

CONSTRUCTION WORKER
Oh, yeah? Lemme show you what I got to share with women.

AMAZON
May you learn from your mistakes.

She makes an adjustment on her transmitter and returns to June.

CONSTRUCTION WORKER
Fuck you, bitch!

The CAMERA FOLLOWS the Amazon and June walking away.

JUNE
You really shouldn't bother with hopeless cases.

AMAZON
Not so hopeless.

There is a FLASH O.S. and a WOMAN'S VOICE calls out.

WOMAN'S VOICE (O.S.)
Hey! HEY! WHAT THE FUCK?!

The Amazon and June turn around.

BY THE CANTEEN TRUCK

The Construction Worker is now a WOMAN CONSTRUCTION WORKER sitting on the ground, dressed in his clothes and holding his Twinkie.

WOMAN CONSTRUCTION WORKER
HEY! WHAT DID YOU DO — WHAT DID YOU DO TO ME?

JUNE AND THE AMAZON

June is amazed -- she begins to laugh. The Amazon takes her arm.

                    AMAZON
    Time to go.

They run off.

BY THE CANTEEN TRUCK

The Woman Construction Worker struggles to her feet, calling after them.

            WOMAN CONSTRUCTION WORKER
    HEY! GET BACK HERE! WHAT THE FUCK DID YOU DO TO ME?!

CONSTRUCTION WORKER #2 walks by, giving him/her the once over. He makes that same nasty KISSING SOUND.

            WOMAN CONSTRUCTION WORKER
    Huh?

                CONSTRUCTION WORKER #2
    New here, baby?

CLOSE SHOT - THE WOMAN CONSTRUCTION WORKER

Shocked and repulsed, the Woman Construction Worker turns and sees his/her reflection in the shiny side of the canteen truck. His/her mouth drops open and he/she drops the Twinkie.

            WOMAN CONSTRUCTION WORKER
    Holy shit!

EXT. DOWN THE STREET FROM THE CONSTRUCTION SITE

The Amazon and June stop. June is out of breath from running and laughing. She grabs the Amazon by her forearms.

                    JUNE
    Oh – that was fantastic! Will he stay a woman?

                    AMAZON
    Just for a while. Long enough.

                    JUNE
    You're amazing.

In a burst of exuberance, she hugs the Amazon. Their faces are very close. June is so attracted to the Amazon it scares her, and she backs off. The Amazon steps aside and gestures with her arm.

                    AMAZON
    Shall we go?

                                        CUT TO:

SERIES OF SHOTS

(NOTE: This is a parody of one of those high-fashion, glitzy numbers -- fast-paced, quick cuts, lush MUSIC UNDER.)

A) June and the Amazon window-shop, arm in arm.

B) The Amazon waves at a naked mannequin.

C) Inside a large department store, the Amazon sniffs perfume.

D) June picks up a pair of socks and turns around, looking for the Amazon.

E) In a three-way mirror, the Amazon is trying on a bra -- she wears the cups on her ass. June, a few feet away, laughs.

F) Together they put on hats.

G) They add gloves and belts.

H) They top off their outfits with leather jackets and pastel umbrellas, look at themselves in a mirror, and on this last mirror shot we:

FREEZE FRAME.

DISSOLVE TO:

INT. A CHINESE RESTAURANT - LUNCHTIME - JUNE'S TABLE

June, the Amazon, and SAL are having lunch. June is arranging her shopping bags at her feet, and Sal is ordering. A WAITER takes their orders.

SAL
- a cup of eggdrop soup and a small shrimp lo mein.

JUNE
That sounds good – I'll have that, too.

AMAZON
Uh, yes – three.

SAL
With a pot of tea.

JUNE
I'll have a glass of white zinfandel. My day off.

WAITER
(to the Amazon)
And for you? What to drink?

AMAZON
Oh – no. I don't – uh – drink.

The Waiter bows and goes off. June gets up.

JUNE
Ladies' room – be right back.
(to the Amazon)
Let Sal tell you about her trip to Sweden.

June reluctantly leaves them alone.

                              SAL
Are you in the program?

                              AMAZON
Hmm?

                              SAL
When you said you didn't drink – I don't mean to pry, I just thought
you might be in the program – AA.

                              AMAZON
                         (unsure but agreeable)
Uh-huh.

                              SAL
Ah – good for you. My lover is – and I don't drink either.
                            (beat)
How long?

                              AMAZON
Hmm?

                              SAL
How LONG?

The Amazon holds her hands apart, guessing.

                              AMAZON
Oh, about a foot –
                        (Sal looks puzzled)
– and a half?
                      (changing the subject)
How was Sweden?

INT. LIZ'S REAL ESTATE OFFICE

Liz isn't eating. She's drinking a diet soda and talking on the phone to her
travel agent.

                              LIZ
                        (on the phone)
Uh-huh ... uh-huh ... well, we wouldn't be interested in that, no.
It must have a balcony overlooking the water ... I can't imagine
anyone going to Puerto Vallarta and not – all right, see what you
can come up with and get back to me.
                      (lowers her voice)
And Jerry – it's love this time. Do you hear what I'm saying? L-U-
S-T spells LOVE. So don't fail me, darling – we *must* have a view.

She hangs up the phone, smugly self-satisfied.

INT. A CHINESE RESTAURANT - JUNE'S TABLE

Sal, June, and the Amazon are eating lunch.

JUNE
(to the Amazon)
Everything okay?

The Amazon nods. She is eating with chopsticks, trying to imitate Sal and June. It's not easy for her.

SAL
You don't have to use those chopsticks.

AMAZON
No?

Relieved, she drops the chopsticks and begins eating her noodles with her fingers.

SAL
No, we can get you a –
(sees the Amazon)
– fork. Or whatever.

June pretends not to notice how the Amazon's eating.

JUNE
(to Sal)
So, go on – have you checked out the sperm banks?

SAL
Oh, a little . . . but what really interests us is the work they've been doing at Vanderbilt, fertilizing one egg with another.

JUNE
So there's no need for sperm.

SAL
Right. And there's a sort of chromosome exchange, so the child gets genes from both mothers.

AMAZON
A form of parthenogenesis.

SAL
Exactly -- and with all X chromosomes, it's always a baby girl.

JUNE
Aww . . . a baby girl who looks like both of you.

SAL
I know – wouldn't that be great? But the research is still very experimental, and the waiting list of women willing to try it is ten miles long . . . by the time they get around to us, I'll be old and gray.
(touching a streak of prematurely gray hair)
Gray-er.

                              JUNE
You want to be the one to carry it?

                              SAL
Oh, definitely. Phyllis could never stand the suspense – besides,
I have the perfect hips for it.
                             (beat)
So, we've got everything – the desire, the stability, the financial
wherewithal, the hips – all we need now is the technology.

June nods sympathetically. The Amazon is wiping her mouth and fingers
on her napkin as she joins in.

                            AMAZON
If the desire is strong enough, you won't need the technology.

                              SAL
What do you mean?

                            AMAZON
The love between you can create your child.

Afraid the Amazon will reveal too much about herself, June treats the subject
lightly.

                             JUNE
Sounds like what my mother used to say – "when you're in love,
God sends you a baby."

                            AMAZON
Yes – she does.

                              SAL
If that's true, why haven't we conceived before now?

                             JUNE
Maybe you've been pushing the wrong buttons.

                            AMAZON
It's not a matter of buttons – it's a matter of positive will.

                             JUNE
                            (aside)
I think she's been reading too much Gordon Liddy.

                              SAL
                        (to the Amazon)
You're serious, aren't you?

                            AMAZON
Because love *is* a miracle, love *makes* miracles.

June smiles sheepishly at Sal, who isn't sure what to think. The Waiter brings
the check and the fortune cookies.

                            WAITER
Will there be anything else?

Julia Willis

                                    JUNE
          No, I think we've had about enough.

The Waiter leaves.

                                     SAL
                                 (intrigued)
          How do you know these things? Who are you?

June hands Sal a fortune cookie.

                                    JUNE
          Here, Sal – get mystic.

                                  AMAZON
                             (answering Sal)
          I'm visiting.

                                     SAL
                            (opening her cookie)
          From which planet?
                            (reading the message)
          Oh my God . . .

                                    JUNE
          What does it say?

                                     SAL
          "Expect a miracle."

June and Sal look at the Amazon who is smiling gently.

EXT. A DOWNTOWN STREET - AFTERNOON

Mary is panhandling on the street. Most people are ignoring her, though she's
hard to ignore.

                                    MARY
          Helping hand here – yoo-hoo – how 'bout a helping hand here?
                               (to a passerby)
          Hey – your mother got a rent-controlled apartment? Huh? Huh?
          If she don't, this is your mother – me – get it? Get it?
                             (shouting after him)
          Yeah, I love you, too!

She gives up and shuffles off into an alley.

EXT. A PARALLEL DOWNTOWN STREET NOT FAR AWAY

June and the Amazon have left Sal at her office and are going back to June's
car. The CAMERA FOLLOWS them.

                                    JUNE
          I just don't think it's fair to go getting her hopes up like that.

                                  AMAZON
          It's not a hope – it's pure creative belief.

                              JUNE
Your belief — not hers. Maybe that's how *you* have babies —

                              AMAZON
Yes, it is.

                              JUNE
Fine — but you can't expect it of Sal and Phyllis.

                              AMAZON
"Expect a miracle."

                              JUNE
You rigged that cookie, too, didn't you?

                              AMAZON
No.
                    (seeing through June)
You're just upset because you didn't tell Sal what's bothering you.

                              JUNE
What could be bothering me? I'm just your average alien tour guide
who's going to have a lot of explaining to do to her friends.

They are walking near an alley in a fairly deserted area. Suddenly, they HEAR
someone calling for help. The Amazon takes off at a run with June following.

EXT. A DOWNTOWN ALLEY

Mary is lying on the ground. ONE THIEF is standing over her with a knife
and a SECOND THIEF in the b.g. is rifling through her bags. Mary is yelling
at the Second Thief.

                              MARY
You get out of my stuff!

                            ONE THIEF
Shut up, old lady, or I cut you.

                          SECOND THIEF
Go on, kill her.

The Amazon runs into the alley and stops. Mary and both Thieves look up.
The Amazon delivers an order.

                             AMAZON
Leave her alone.

The Thief with the knife takes a step away from Mary and toward the Amazon.

                              MARY
Look out — he'll stick you.

The Amazon touches her transmitter and stretches out her arm. June arrives behind her just in time to see first One Thief and then the Second Thief freeze like statues. The Amazon walks over to Mary to help her up.

After staring at the frozen Thief with the knife, June joins them and collects Mary's bags -- she has to jerk one bag out of the Second Thief's frozen grasp. Mary is dumbfounded.

AMAZON
(helping Mary up)

It's all right.

MARY

Holy Mary on a graham cracker – what did you do to 'em? Why ain't they moving?

AMAZON

I've stopped them.

MARY

I'll say.

She takes a good look at the Amazon and recognizes the Escapee.

MARY
(continuing)

Hey – it's you! Where'd you get them clothes – why ain't you hiding? Say, what is all this – "Candid Camera?"

AMAZON
(referring to her wrist transmitter)

No, it isn't a camera.

MARY

Huh?

June puts Mary's bags down in front of her.

JUNE

Here – is this all?

MARY
(to June)

Why has this girl been following me?

JUNE

I don't know – she's been following me, too.

She gives Mary a twenty-dollar bill and a business card.

JUNE
(continuing)

Please, take this – and my card. I'm with Project Share.

MARY

Yeah, I know the place.

(to the Amazon)

But why are you – ?

                              JUNE
Can we take you to a hospital? Drop you anywhere?

                              MARY
No, no — I'm all right.
                          (to the Amazon)
You going with *her*?

                             AMAZON
Yes.

                              MARY
                           (shrugging)
Okay. Whatever.

                              JUNE
If you need help, call that number. Good luck.

June and the Amazon start away. Mary calls to the Amazon.

                              MARY
Hey! When will these guys be moving again?

                             AMAZON
                        (over her shoulder)
Never.

June and the Amazon exit.

                              MARY
Oh.

                            (beat)
Good.

She approaches one of the frozen Thieves and proceeds to pick his pockets.

INT. A WOMEN'S BAR - MID-AFTERNOON

The bar is almost empty. The BARTENDER is pouring a glass of wine. June
and the Amazon are sitting on stools at the bar. June tries to understand
how the Amazon froze those men in their tracks.

                              JUNE
Mo-lec-u-lar manipulation.

                             AMAZON
And their negative actions made them particularly vulnerable to my
re-action . . . does that make it any clearer?

                              JUNE
It's like turning that guy into a woman.

                             AMAZON
Yes — but that was playing. Those others were dangerous.

The Bartender serves June her wine. June raises the glass.

Julia Willis

                    JUNE
Well, they're not anymore. God, I feel empowered! I wish we could
toast to – isn't there anything you can drink?

                    AMAZON
I don't know.
                    (looking at June's glass)
Isn't that what you had at lunch?

                    JUNE
Wine.

                    AMAZON
May I taste it?

                    JUNE
Oh, I don't know . . .

But June gives the Amazon the glass and she puts it to her lips. She sniffs
it and takes a tiny sip.

                    AMAZON
Mmm . . . not bad.
                    (another sip)
Oh, I like that.

                    JUNE
Careful.

                    AMAZON
                    (a bigger sip)
I think this might be all right.

The Amazon tilts her head back and gulps down the wine. She puts down
the glass and sighs appreciatively.

                    AMAZON
Ahh . . .

June is watching her for any signs of inebriation.

                    JUNE
Feeling okay?

                    AMAZON
Fine.

Suddenly, the Amazon drops her head down on the bar. June calls to her
as the Bartender looks on.

                    JUNE
Dawn!

Just as quickly the Amazon raises her head and smiles.

                    AMAZON
Kidding.

JUNE

Oh.
                 (to the Bartender)
She's all right – she was just being silly.

                 AMAZON
                 (to the Bartender)
I was just being silly.

The Bartender doesn't seem to have much of a sense of humor. June points
to her empty glass.

                 JUNE
Well – I guess we'll have two more of these.

The Bartender leaves.

                 JUNE
                 (continuing; to the Amazon)
That wasn't very nice.

                 AMAZON
I'm sorry.

                 JUNE
I'll forgive you if you'll show me how to manipulate molecules.

                 AMAZON
Oh, I see. I shouldn't teach things to Sal, but I can teach them
to you.

                 JUNE
But that's vital information. Think what I could do –

                 AMAZON
Sal's child is vital to her.

                 JUNE
Yeah . . .

                 AMAZON
Also much easier to create. I couldn't teach you the other. It requires
energy you don't have – especially on this planet, where you're
constantly counteracting negativity.

                 JUNE
So I can't learn how to freeze people?

The Bartender serves them and, overhearing June's last remark, gives her
a strange look.

                 JUNE
                 (continuing)
Why don't we move to a table?

INT. NANCY'S OFFICE

Nancy is still at her desk, eating yogurt. Phyllis enters with a yellow legal pad in her hand.

> PHYLLIS
> You rang?

> NANCY
> Yeah — I wanted to apologize for this morning.

> PHYLLIS
> Not necessary. I didn't mean to overhear your call, and I won't ask any more questions.

> NANCY
> (confessing)
> I'm having an affair.

Phyllis sits across from Nancy, making a note on her pad and trying to appear casual.

> PHYLLIS
> Well ... anyone we know?

> NANCY
> Former client — Liz Nardone.

> PHYLLIS
> (not recalling the name)
> Sex discrimination case?

> NANCY
> No.

> PHYLLIS
> Surely not a divorce?

> NANCY
> No. Real estate matter.

> PHYLLIS
> Since when are you interested in real estate?

> NANCY
> I've been seriously considering going into real estate law.

> PHYLLIS
> With a new partner, I assume.

> NANCY
> Phyl — it's just something I'm thinking about ... but I thought I ought to warn you.

> PHYLLIS
> Thanks. Who's warning June?

Nancy looks guilty.

INT. A WOMEN'S BAR - A TABLE IN THE CORNER

June and the Amazon are sitting at a table. An hour has passed. June has had several glasses of wine. So has the Amazon, but it hasn't affected her.

JUNE

So – that was my childhood.
(beat)
Are you sure you don't want to go to a movie or take a walk in the park or something?

AMAZON

I'll do whatever you'd like, June.

There is a moment of sexual tension, as June looks into the Amazon's eyes. She swallows hard.

JUNE

Oh, gosh, I don't know – can you give me a ride in your ship? Or tell me what life must be like in a land without nuclear weapons and violent crime – and lies – and deception?
(beat)
Isn't this crazy? I mean, this is probably the most important day of my life, and here I sit – it's crazy. Isn't it?

AMAZON

No.

JUNE

(after a pause)
You were right about Sal ... I did want to talk to her – about something.
(putting it into words)
I think Nancy's seeing someone else.
(beat)
How about another drink?

AMAZON

I think we've had enough.

June almost allows herself to be angry.

JUNE

I guess what really pisses me off – I'm letting my own damn personal issues get in the way of having a really memorable day with you.

AMAZON

(as a question)
And you shouldn't?

JUNE

(hearing it as a fact)
No. I shouldn't. You're absolutely right.

June gets up, a little unsteadily.

                              JUNE
                          (continuing)
We're going home, and I'm going to make you a memorable dinner,
and then we'll have a memorable evening in front of a memorable
fire – and if Nancy doesn't wish to join us, too bad. Come on.

The Amazon goes along, taking June's car keys out of her hand.

                              AMAZON
You'd better let me drive.

                              JUNE
Can you drive my car?

                              AMAZON
We'll find out.

                              JUNE
A memorable drive! Let's go!
                          (to the Bartender)
We're off to see the Wizard!

                              AMAZON
The Wizard!

The Bartender shakes her head.

EXT. UNDER A SET OF STEPS DOWNTOWN - CLOSE SHOT - THE
ESCAPEE

The Escapee is hiding where Mary left her, dozing. She wakes abruptly out
of a dream.

                              ESCAPEE
The Wizard!
                          (hearing herself)
Huh?

She wonders why she just said that -- was she dreaming? Then we HEAR
Mary O.S. as she is coming down the street.

                              MARY (O.S.)
There you are! I can't believe it! You oughta see those guys! You're
a wonder, kid, I don't know how you did it!

                              ESCAPEE
Huh?

TWO SHOT - MARY AND THE ESCAPEE

Mary comes under the steps to join her, cackling with laughter.

                              MARY
Oh, it cracks me up! Stiff as a coupla boards – like something
out of a Vincent Price picture – wax dummies – you gotta tell me
how you did it!

Amazon X   159

ESCAPEE
Did what?

Mary takes out a roll of bills.

MARY
And what'd you think? I took maybe four hundred bucks off those
creeps – they were loaded.
(giving the Escapee half)
Here – I'm splitting it with you. It's only fair.

ESCAPEE
(hesitant)
It is?

MARY
Sure. You know, I been thinking – between you and me, we could
set us up a nice little racket ...

Mary winds down a notch and takes a closer look at the Escapee.

MARY
(continuing)
Say – that was *you*, wasn't it?

ESCAPEE
(confused)
I don't know what you're talking about.

MARY
(also confused)
So you weren't – you didn't – and they froze up like popsicles?
(beat)
Jeez ... maybe it *was* "Candid Camera."

EXT. JUNE'S MOVING CAR - LONG SHOT

The Amazon drives June's car, slightly erratically but very well -- almost as
if they were airborne.

INT. JUNE AND NANCY'S HOUSE - LIVING ROOM - LATE AFTERNOON

June and the Amazon come in with shopping bags.

JUNE
Oh, it was just like flying!

AMAZON
Not quite.

June flops down on the couch. The Amazon flops, too.

JUNE
I must be the luckiest woman in the world.

AMAZON
In this world?

                              JUNE
In *any* world.

She looks at the clock.

                              JUNE
                           (continuing)
Oh – look at the time. Time to start the sauce. I'm making my
special spaghetti sauce – if you like Italian for breakfast, you'll love
it for dinner.
                            (thinking)
Hmm ... I don't have any fresh mushrooms. Or garlic. I don't
suppose you can manifest mushrooms and garlic?

The Amazon shakes her head. June gets up again.

                              JUNE
                           (continuing)
No problem – I'll run to the store. In fact, I'll walk – it's good for
me. Coming?

                             AMAZON
I'd rather stay here and stand in your shower.

                              JUNE
Make yourself at home, dear.

June pauses at the door.

                              JUNE
                           (continuing)
God, you're beautiful.

The Amazon laughs in surprise.

INTERCUT - INT. NANCY'S OFFICE/LIZ'S OFFICE

Nancy is on the phone with Liz again. She sounds a little strained.

                             NANCY
                         (on the phone)
That sounds great – I'll have two weeks coming.

                              LIZ
                         (on the phone)
I'll make all the arrangements. Dorothy will whisk you away to Oz.
All you have to do is lie back and enjoy it.
                          (no response)
Darling?

                             NANCY
I've decided to speak to June tonight ... about us. I don't know
how she'll take it, but I have to be honest.

                              LIZ
                           (soothing)
Of course – because you *are* so honest. I love that about you.

Amazon X   161

NANCY
I may not be able to call you later – I'll have to play it by ear.

LIZ
Do whatever you think's best, darling.

NANCY
I will.
(beat)
I love you.

LIZ
Oh, and I love you ...

Nancy hangs up and takes a deep breath, preparing to go home and tell June.

END ON LIZ

Liz leans back in her chair contentedly.

EXT. DOWNTOWN STREET

We DOLLY with Mary and the Escapee as they walk along. Mary is insisting the Escapee keep half the money she took off the thieves. She pats the Escapee's pocket.

MARY
Come on, keep the dough – whoever she was, she had to be a relative of yours. Got a sister?

The Escapee shakes her head.

MARY
(continuing)
Aunt? Cousin? Any family?

ESCAPEE
(roughly)
No!

MARY
Okay, okay.
(changing the subject)
So – how's about dinner? Anything you want – it's on me. How 'bout a burger and a big thick shake? Or clams – you like clams?

The Escapee touches her body and looks up at the sky -- she can feel water coming down, but it isn't really there.

ESCAPEE
Is it raining?

MARY
Nah – that's spit. My mouth's watering like crazy. You like a big thick steak?

Julia Willis

INT. JUNE AND NANCY'S BATHROOM - MED. SHOT - THE AMAZON

The Amazon is showering, as if she were under a waterfall, very natural and playful.

DISSOLVE TO:

EXT. THE AMAZON'S PLANET - DAY - FULL SHOT - WATERFALL

The Amazon stands under a real waterfall with several other AMAZONS like her. The SOUND OF RUSHING WATER is accompanied by their LAUGHTER.

CUT TO:

INT. JUNE AND NANCY'S LIVING ROOM

The Amazon walks naked (except for her wrist transmitter) into the living room where she left her spacesuit and boots. She is wiping off her face and toweling her hair a little with a hand towel, but the rest of her body is dripping wet.

The PHONE RINGS. The Amazon picks it up and holds the receiver against her ear carefully.

> AMAZON
> (on the phone)
> Um – I greet you.

INT. LIZ'S OFFICE - SAME TIME

It's Liz calling from her office. She is feeling so bold and reckless now that she's calling Nancy at home.

> LIZ
> (on the phone)
> May I speak to Nancy, please?

INTERCUT THE AMAZON AND LIZ

> AMAZON
> Um – Nancy isn't here now.

> LIZ
> Oh? I just spoke to her.

> AMAZON
> Over a telephone?

> LIZ
> Not with two tin cans and a string.
> (beat)
> I guess she was still at the office.
> (really pushing it)
> Is this – June?

> AMAZON
> No.

The Amazon realizes the party she is speaking to is "The Other Woman."

> **AMAZON**
> **(continuing)**
> This is Dawn Brillo.

Liz pauses, thinking "what a weird name."

> **LIZ**
> Right ... okay, would you give Nancy a message, please?

The Amazon is fiddling with her transmitter and scratching her nose while holding the receiver against her shoulder. (Hmm -- what does she have in mind for Liz?)

> **AMAZON**
> Yes.

> **LIZ**
> Just tell her "Dorothy" called from Oz -- to wish her luck. Can you do that?

> **AMAZON**
> I certainly can, my pretty.

> **LIZ**
> **(with a laugh)**
> Thanks. Ciao.

Liz hangs up. The Amazon finishes adjusting her transmitter and puts down the receiver.

END ON THE AMAZON

> **AMAZON**
> **(looking at the phone)**
> And your little dog, too.

Nancy comes in at that very moment and finds the Amazon standing naked and wet in her living room. She's shocked.

> **NANCY**
> Wha -- ?

> **AMAZON**
> I'm still here.

> **NANCY**
> Yes, I can see that. Am I interrupting anything -- should I come back later?

> **AMAZON**
> No -- I'm finished. I had to wash. It's very dirty here.

> **NANCY**
> **(sarcastic)**
> Thanks.

You're welcome.

Nancy goes to her desk and puts down her briefcase.

NANCY
You're dripping all over the floor.

AMAZON
Oh. Sorry.

The Amazon crouches down to wipe the floor with her hand towel. Nancy glances toward the bedroom.

NANCY
Where's June – is she dripping, too?

AMAZON
No.
(standing up again)
I have a message for you.

NANCY
From June?

She raises her voice, thinking June is in the house.

NANCY
(continuing)
Something she can't tell me herself?

AMAZON
From Dorothy.

NANCY
Who?

AMAZON
Dorothy – in Oz. She called to wish you luck.

NANCY
(realizing that's Liz)
Oh. When did she call?

AMAZON
Just now.

June enters with a bag of groceries and sees the wet Amazon first. She begins to laugh.

JUNE
Oh, dear – didn't you see the towels?

AMAZON
(holds up the hand towel)
This?

                              JUNE
        Oh ... what am I gonna do with − ?

June sees Nancy. Nancy figures her best defense is a good offense.

                             NANCY
        Would you like to explain what's going on here?

June is still a little high and doesn't like Nancy's tone one bit.

                              JUNE
        I'm going to make dinner − what do you think's going on here?

Nancy points accusingly at the Amazon.

                             NANCY
        I think there is someone without her clothes on dripping all over
        the floor when she knows I asked her to leave my house this morning.

                              JUNE
                         (raising her voice)
        She is *my* guest in *our* house and she can drip anywhere she wants
        to.

                            AMAZON
        I'll go outside and drip.

The Amazon starts for the door.

                             NANCY
        Hey − not like that you won't.

                              JUNE
        Put your suit on, Dawn.

                            AMAZON
        Oh − sure.

June goes with her bag into the kitchen. Nancy follows her. The Amazon
begins to dress.

INT. JUNE AND NANCY'S KITCHEN

A continuation of the previous scene. June unpacks the bag of groceries
-- garlic, mushrooms, angel hair pasta, two bottles of wine, fresh candles, etc.

                              JUNE
        So − you kicked her out this morning, huh?

                             NANCY
        I told you how I felt about her.

                              JUNE
        You told me she was some sort of criminal − which she is not.

                             NANCY
        Then what *is* she?

---

166   Julia Willis

JUNE
(knowing Nancy won't believe her)
She's a visitor from another planet.

NANCY
If you won't be serious, I can't talk to you.

JUNE
Okay, don't believe me – but it's the truth.

NANCY
Well, that might explain why she runs around naked all the time.

JUNE
Some women are just naturally uninhibited about their bodies.

NANCY
Great – and every time I walk into my own house I think I'm at a goddam women's music festival.

EXT. JUNE AND NANCY'S FRONT PORCH

The Amazon is swinging in the porch swing with her eyes closed.

INT. A VINYL BOOTH IN A CHEAP RESTAURANT

Mary and the Escapee are looking at menus. The Escapee begins to rock back and forth, as if she's in a porch swing.

MARY
Ah, now we're cookin' ... gee, I can't decide – it all looks good.
(notices the Escapee)
Hey – what's with the hobbyhorse bit?

ESCAPEE
(puzzled)
I don't know.

MARY
Tone it down – I don't want to get thrown out of here till I'm stuffed like a porkchop ... you like porkchops?

The Escapee grabs the table to stop rocking.

ESCAPEE
Mary – is there a church around here?

MARY
Never pray on an empty stomach, kid.

INT. JUNE AND NANCY'S KITCHEN

Preparations for dinner are coming along. June has a knife in her hand to cut up mushrooms. Nancy closes the refrigerator door.

NANCY
Still no beer.

I'm making spaghetti – we're having wine. Are you staying for dinner, or do you have other plans?

Nancy picks up one of the bottles of wine.

NANCY

Vintage stock – la-de-da. What sort of plans do *you* have?

June chops mushrooms angrily.

JUNE

Oh, shut up!

NANCY

I was going to be here for dinner, but now I don't know.

JUNE

Okay – when you decide, you can set the table.

NANCY
(serious)
I was hoping we could sit down and talk tonight.

JUNE

Really? What a coincidence – I've been hoping that for weeks.

NANCY

We won't be able to if she's here.

JUNE

Then we'll just have to put it off, won't we?

NANCY

Just how long is she staying?

JUNE

Just as long as she wants.
(beat; sincerely)
Nance, she's a miracle – she makes me think there's still hope for the world ... if not ours, then at least someone's.

NANCY

Did you sleep with her?

After all June's suspicions about Nancy, and her attraction to the Amazon which she has tried not to act on, this is the last straw.

JUNE

Not yet. But if I do, you'll be the first to know.

NANCY

Is that supposed to make it all right?

June puts down her knife.

                              JUNE
I have never lied to you, and I never will. Now – is there anything
you'd like to tell *me*?

Nancy is guilty, confused, jealous -- she chickens out.

                             NANCY
I can't talk to you with that woman in the house.

                              JUNE
She isn't *in* the house – she went outside.

                             NANCY
I still have nothing to say.

                              JUNE
Then don't say it.

June goes back to chopping mushrooms. Nancy again takes the offensive,
preparing to leave.

                             NANCY
I don't know what's going on, and I don't care – but I don't have
to sit here and watch it.
                             (beat)
Do whatever you want.

                              JUNE
Thanks. I will.

                             NANCY
I won't be home tonight.

                              JUNE
If you change your mind, be sure and call first.

Nancy goes. June got the last word -- but she has mixed feelings about the
fight; she knows now that Nancy must be having an affair -- she also know
she wants to make love with the Amazon.

EXT. JUNE AND NANCY'S FRONT PORCH AND YARD - STILL LATE
AFTERNOON

The Amazon is sitting on the swing. Neighbor Doris is walking by in her
nurse's uniform carrying a paper bag. She speaks to the Amazon.

                             DORIS
Hello. Feeling better?

                            AMAZON
Yes, thank you.

EXT. DORIS AND BETTY'S YARD NEXT DOOR

Doris waves and walks into her yard where BETTY, her "long-time companion,"
is gardening. She hands Betty the bag.

Amazon X   169

> **DORIS**
>
> Hi, honey.

> **BETTY**
>
> Oh, good — you remembered my fertilizer.

> **DORIS**
>
> Of course.

Next door Nancy comes storming out of the house, slamming the door, and goes straight to her car without a word to the Amazon. As she drives away, the Amazon gets up and goes into the house. Doris and Betty watch.

> **BETTY**
>
> Ah — and they were such a nice couple.

> **DORIS**
>
> Kids today — they don't know the meaning of commitment.

She puts her arm around Betty's shoulder.

INT. LIZ'S LIVING ROOM

Liz has just gotten home. She throws a stack of travel folders on the coffee table. A funny look comes over her face and she begins to scratch her shoulder. She's getting a strange itch, courtesy of the Amazon.

INT. JUNE AND NANCY'S KITCHEN

The Amazon comes into the kitchen. June is cooking and sniffling. She's been crying a little.

> **JUNE**
>
> Hi. Hope you're hungry — there'll just be two for dinner.

> **AMAZON**
>
> I'm sorry, June.

> **JUNE**
>
> Oh, it's not your fault — we've been headed this way for months ... now at least I know the truth.

> **AMAZON**
>
> She told you, then.

> **JUNE**
>
> She did everything *but* tell me — did you already know?

> **AMAZON**
>
> That Nancy has someone else? Yes, I — sensed it.

> **JUNE**
>
> So did I. I don't know how she thought she could keep it from me.

> **AMAZON**
>
> We can't hide the way we feel.

---

170   Julia Willis

June looks at the Amazon, thinking of the way she feels.

                    JUNE
Guess not.

She hands the Amazon a glass of wine and shows her how to clink their glasses together in a toast.

                    JUNE
                  (continuing)
To a lovely evening.

                    AMAZON
                (gazing at June)
To a lovely woman.

For a moment June looks as if she might cry again -- then she begins to smile instead.

INT. LIZ'S LIVING ROOM

The RADIO is PLAYING oldies' rock 'n roll. Clothes and travel folders are scattered around the living room.

There's a KNOCK at the door. Liz, not expecting company, comes out of the kitchen in a ratty terry cloth bathrobe, eating pasta salad out of the store container.

                    LIZ
Who is it?

                 NANCY (O.S.)
It's me.

                    LIZ
Oh!

She clutches at her robe and looks around the room -- it's such a mess she doesn't know where to start.

                 NANCY (O.S.)
                  (waiting)
Liz?

                    LIZ
Yes — yes.

Liz realizes she can't leave Nancy standing outside while she cleans up --so she gives in and opens the door.

                    LIZ
Well ... is this my surprise?

Nancy steps inside, recalling the balloon surprise she's ordered for Liz.

                    NANCY
Oh — no. I'm sorry, I probably should have called first ...

LIZ

No, darling, don't ever feel you can't come over --

She sees Nancy surveying the room in such a mess.

LIZ
(continuing)
-- but of course I wasn't expecting anyone.
(clutching at her robe)
I haven't even showered.

NANCY
(helpless)
I just didn't know where else to go.

LIZ

Oh, come here.

She takes Nancy in her arms, still holding her pasta salad in one hand.

NANCY

I walked out.

LIZ

Poor baby.
(a gleam in her eye)
So you told her.

NANCY

She's already moving someone else in.

Liz holds Nancy at arm's length, thinking of her phone conversation with the Amazon.

LIZ

Oh -- that Dawn somebody?

NANCY
(genuinely jealous)
That's who she says she is -- I don't know who she is or where she comes from, but June's -- she's falling for the woman -- it's obvious.

LIZ

But that's good, don't you see? It makes things so much easier for everybody.

NANCY
(unsure)
Yeah ...

Nancy notices a piece of salad stuck between Liz's teeth.

Julia Willis

                              NANCY
                           (continuing)
        You have a little –
                        (picks at her own tooth)
        – on your tooth.

                               LIZ
                          (embarrassed)
        Oh.

Liz removes it quickly. Things suddenly seem awkward between them. Nancy
looks at the pasta salad.

                              NANCY
                            (hungry)
        Is that your dinner?

                               LIZ
                            (polite)
        Yes – would you like some?

                              NANCY
                          (also polite)
        Do you have enough?

                               LIZ
                            (lying)
        Of course.

Nancy takes the salad and begins to eat as she heads for the couch. She
continues to obsess about June.

                              NANCY
        Mmm ... good.
                             (beat)
        But she only met the woman yesterday – it's all so sudden ...

Liz joins her on the couch, nodding sympathetically and scratching herself
in several more places while Nancy devours her supper.

EXT. OUTSIDE A DOWNTOWN CHURCH - NIGHT

Mary and the Escapee arrive at the front doors -- Mary is sucking on a toothpick.
The Escapee tries first one door, then the other. Both doors are locked.

                              MARY
        Told you – they always keep 'em locked, except when somebody's
        there to rake in the dough.

The Escapee sits on the steps dejectedly. Mary joins her.

                              MARY
                           (continuing)
        Ah, those pews are too hard to sleep on, anyway.

ESCAPEE
(after a pause)
Mary — I think there's an angel calling me. Is that crazy?

MARY
Hey — to each his own.

ESCAPEE
(another pause)
He says I tried to kill him.

MARY
Who — the angel?

ESCAPEE
(confessing)
No. Dennis.
(beat)
But I wasn't trying to — was I? I just wanted to leave — I just
wanted out.
(beat)
So I shot him. Now if they catch me they'll lock me up. I can't
be locked up anymore.
(crying)
I only wanted out, Mary ... I'm not crazy, I'm not crazy — I just
don't belong here.

Mary puts the Escapee's head in her lap and comforts her.

MARY
Sure, that's all right. Nobody with any sense belongs here.

ESCAPEE
I've been thinking I should take this gun and shoot myself.

MARY
Nah, you don't want to do that — very messy.

ESCAPEE
What am I going to do?

MARY
Ask that angel, kid — she'll give it to you straight.

INT. LIZ'S LIVING ROOM

Nancy is still obsessing about June and the Amazon, and Liz is itching all
over now.

NANCY
I told June I wouldn't be coming home.

LIZ
(scratching her leg)
Darling — we'll have the whole night together.

                        NANCY
    She's going to sleep with that woman – I just know it.
                        (beat)
    And who *is* she – this "Dawn?" They just met – June knows nothing
    about her . . .

Liz is trying to reassure Nancy and scratch her itching back at the same time.

                        LIZ
    She sounded all right on the phone.

                        NANCY
                        (sharply)
    You can't tell what someone's like over the phone.

                        LIZ
    Excuse me – I was merely making a comment.

                        NANCY
    I'm sorry.

Nancy finally notices the way Liz is itching and scratching.

                        NANCY
    Why are you scratching like that?

                        LIZ
    There! If you'd been paying any attention to me, that's what you
    would've said ten minutes ago.

                        NANCY
    Well, what's wrong?

                        LIZ
    I don't know!
                        (examining her arm)
    I can't see anything, I can't feel any lumps – it just itches!

Liz tries desperately to scratch her back again. Nancy steps in to help.

                        NANCY
    Here, let me –

                        LIZ
                        (directing her)
    Up, up – to the left, to the left – THE LEFT!

                        NANCY
    Your left or my left?

                        LIZ
    It's all the same fucking LEFT!

The DOORBELL RINGS.

                        LIZ
                        (continuing)
    Oh, you're just making it worse!

Amazon X   175

She gets up to answer the door.

                              LIZ
                         (continuing)
        This won't be June, I hope.

                            NANCY
        Oh, no, it couldn't be — I haven't told her about you yet.

                              LIZ
                          (surprised)
        You haven't told her?

                            NANCY
        I didn't get a chance.

                              LIZ
        Then what is all this about? Are you just here to cry on my shoulder
        because *she's* having an affair?

                            NANCY
        No — I'm sure she knows something. Dawn must've told her.

The DOORBELL RINGS again. Liz calls to the door.

                              LIZ
        Just a minute!
                          (to Nancy)
        What does Dawn know — what did you tell her?

                            NANCY
        Nothing. She guessed. She knew I'd been with you when I went
        home last night.

                              LIZ
        And how did she know that?

                            NANCY
                         (being honest)
        She said she could smell you.

                              LIZ
                          (insulted)
        Oh, that's great, that's terrific — I itch, and I smell.

                            NANCY
        No, Liz, she just says these things — she's weird. I don't know
        what June's doing with somebody like that.

                              LIZ
        So what am I supposed to think — that I've got the mange?

The DOORBELL RINGS a third time. Liz flings the door open.

                              LIZ
                         (continuing)
        WHAT *IS* IT?

A BALLOON GIRL in a white tuxedo is standing at the door with a huge bunch of lavender balloons.

BALLOON GIRL
(checking her card)
Elizabeth Nardone?

Liz, still scratching, explodes when she sees the balloons.

LIZ
Oh! Whose idea of a joke is this? I hate balloons! I hate them – they blow up in my face! Get them out of here!

The Balloon Girl stands there, not knowing what to do.

LIZ
Nancy, darling, please, get rid of her – I can't stand this – I'm going to take a bath!

Liz leaves the room. As Nancy comes to the door, the Balloon Girl blows on a pitch pipe and attempts to sing "OVER THE RAINBOW."

BALLOON GIRL
"Some-where –"

NANCY
Thank you.

Her surprise ruined, Nancy closes the door in the Balloon Girl's face.

INT. JUNE AND NANCY'S LIVING ROOM

June and the Amazon have finished dinner and are lying in front of a cozy little fire, harmonizing.

JUNE/THE AMAZON
(together)
"Da-da land da-da-da-da, da-da-da lullaby ... "

The PHONE RINGS. June groans.

JUNE
Oh, I don't want to get that.

AMAZON
Shall I? I know how.

The Amazon gets up to answer the phone.

JUNE
If it's Nancy, I can't talk to her.

AMAZON
(on the phone)
I greet you.
(beat)
Oh, yes.
(telling June)
This is Sal.

June's a little disappointed it isn't Nancy.

                              JUNE
          Oh.

She holds out her hand for the receiver.

                              AMAZON
                         (on the phone)
          Yes ... uh-huh ...
                         (telling June)
          She wants to ask me something.

June puts her hand back down.

                              JUNE
          Oh.

                              AMAZON
                         (on the phone)
          Go ahead ... uh-huh ... uh-huh ... uh-huh ... uh-huh.
                         (answering Sal)
          Yes, you can – tonight – yes, I will – and it will look like both
          of you.
                              (beat)
          Yes ... good-bye. Love.

She hangs up and sits down with June.

                              AMAZON
                      (continuing; casually)
          They're going to have a baby.

                              JUNE
          Just like that?

                              AMAZON
          I'm helping.

                              JUNE
                   (referring to the wrist transmitter)
          With your magic decoder ring?

                              AMAZON
          No – just my thoughts.

                              JUNE
          How – like praying? I mean, will you have to go off somewhere
          and do it?

                              AMAZON
          I'm doing it now.

She takes June's hand.

                              AMAZON
                         (continuing)
          I'm not going anywhere.

Julia Willis

JUNE
(afraid of her feelings)
I – uh – forgot dessert.

AMAZON
Don't be afraid, June.

June takes her hand away.

JUNE
I think this is where I'm supposed to say "Gee, I'm just really confused and I need to be alone tonight."

AMAZON
Do you?

JUNE
No, but –

AMAZON
Go on – you may ask.

JUNE
Okay . . . this is probably a dumb – well, is this really you? I mean, is this what you look like all over – and underneath?

AMAZON
(smiling)
This is what I have always looked like – except as a child I was much smaller.

JUNE
(relieved)
Oh, good . . . I kept wondering if you could be a slime creature or something. Not that looks are all that important – but I think I'd have to draw the line at slime.

AMAZON
We all have our preferences. Anything else?

JUNE
(after a pause)
I've always been faithful to Nancy.
(beat)
Intimacy's not a game with me – it has to mean something.

AMAZON
I know.

JUNE
The way you travel, the way you look, I can't help thinking I could be just another – well, are you the type who has a girl in every galaxy?

AMAZON
(laughing)
No. I draw the line long before slime creatures.
(MORE)

AMAZON (cont'd)
(beat)
I rarely meet my subjects of study – and I've *never* met anyone like you.

JUNE
(overwhelmed)
Oh dear.

AMAZON
June, why do you think I've wanted to be with you? Yes, there are other reasons I'm here – but you ... you are so very special.

JUNE
Oh – and you're –

June moves into the Amazon's arms and kisses her. The Amazon reclines on her back and lets June roll on top of her, as they continue kissing. Then June stops.

JUNE
Hey – we aren't making a baby, are we?

AMAZON
Not this time.

JUNE
Probably best – joint custody would be awfully hard on her.

AMAZON
Six months in your universe, six months in mine?

They laugh and kiss again, as June rolls over on her back. Finally, the Amazon sits up.

AMAZON
The fire is dying.
(holding out her hand)
Come.

She leads June toward the bedroom.

INT. LIZ'S BEDROOM

Nancy and Liz are sitting in the bed. Nancy is wearing a tanktop with the covers up to her waist. She has brought her bottle of champagne from the night before to bed and is drinking it.

Liz is naked to the waist, with a box of Kleenex on her lap. She uses a hand mirror to look for spots on her face and body and dabs at them with calamine lotion on a tissue. She is practically covered in blobs of cakey pink lotion.

Nancy offers Liz her glass.

NANCY
Champagne?

LIZ
(irritable)
I only have two hands, don't I?

NANCY
(bored)
Is there anything to read around here?

LIZ
There's a whole pile of magazines over there in the closet.

NANCY
I didn't mean magazines, I meant books.

LIZ
Oh — pardon me.

NANCY
How about a newspaper?

LIZ
I left it at work.

NANCY
(incredulous)
And you don't have *any* books?

LIZ
What do I look like, a librarian?

Liz proceeds to go on dabbing calamine lotion, and Nancy sits holding her glass of champagne.

NANCY
All right — then tell me about Puerto Vallarta.

LIZ
You don't seem to realize how horribly I'm itching — it's unbearable.

NANCY
But there's nothing there.

LIZ
You think I'm making it up, is that it?

NANCY
I didn't —

LIZ
That just shows how little you know me.
(beat)
And we're not going to Puerto Vallarta. It's entirely too ordinary — Jerry says New Zealand is the place this year. I brought home some travel folders, you should go and get them.

NANCY
New Zealand? That must cost a fortune.

LIZ
We can do two full weeks for under four thousand – each. Maybe.

NANCY
I can't afford that.

LIZ
Of course you can – charge it.

NANCY
I wouldn't do that.

LIZ
Sure you would – that's what credit's for.
(itching)
Oh, I can't stand it!

NANCY
I can't possibly go to New Zealand right now.

LIZ
All right – forget it! I don't want to discuss it!

NANCY
Neither do I.
(beat)
Some evening.

LIZ
(launching into a speech)
Well, Nancy, I really don't know what you expect. You come over
without calling, you eat *my* dinner, you send me those awful balloons
(which was a sweet thought but which unfortunately I loathe and
despise), you have no spirit of adventure and apparently no grasp
of the concept that this country *exists* on its charge cards – and
now you want me to entertain you when I'm positively covered in
calamine lotion.
(beat)
Maybe you'd better just go home.

NANCY
(pouting)
I can't go home – June's not expecting me.

LIZ
Oh, well – let's not inconvenience June.

Nancy gets out of bed, takes her champagne and her clothes and heads for
the living room.

NANCY
I'll be on the couch. If you need anything, *don't* whistle.

She walks out, and Liz makes a face after her before going back to itching
and dabbing lotion.

Julia Willis

INT. SAL AND PHYLLIS'S BEDROOM

Sal and Phyllis are in bed. They've made love and now they're cuddling.

SAL

How do you feel?

PHYLLIS

Now I know what they mean by performance anxiety.

Sal smacks her playfully.

PHYLLIS
(continuing)
No, really – in all our many nights of exquisite passion, this is
the first time I ever had to think about what we were doing ...
and frankly, I was shocked.

Phyllis grabs Sal and hugs her tightly.

PHYLLIS
(continuing)
I feel like a bowl of fresh whipped cream – how do you feel?

SAL
(softly)
I feel like a mother.

PHYLLIS

Not your mother, I hope.

SAL

No, I mean it, Phyl. I think I – that I'm –

PHYLLIS

You mean – ?
(a little skeptical)
No ... how can you tell?

SAL

I don't know, I just –

Phyllis becomes concerned and excited.

PHYLLIS
Honey, I think it's too soon to – isn't it?

SAL
I just never felt this way before.

PHYLLIS
Really? Truly? Honestly?

SAL
(nodding)
Phyl –

PHYLLIS
Yes, precious, what can I do?

SAL
Get me a pickle.

Sal bursts out laughing and Phyllis grabs a pillow and socks her with it. They collapse in one another's arms, laughing.

INT. JUNE AND NANCY'S BEDROOM

June and the Amazon make love.

EXT. THE DOWNTOWN CHURCH STEPS

Mary and the Escapee are huddled on the steps, sleeping. Mary is snoring. The Escapee wakes and sits up -- a shiver of pleasure not unlike an orgasm runs through her. She looks as if she's had a vision. She shakes Mary gently.

ESCAPEE
Mary – Mary –

MARY
(stirring)
Ah – lemme sleep.

ESCAPEE
Mary – we're getting out of here.

MARY
Swell – lemme sleep.

ESCAPEE
Where do you want to go?

MARY
(her eyes closed)
Florida.

ESCAPEE
Okay ... and I'll go –
(struggling to see it)
– far, far away. Behind the moon, beyond the rain ...

MARY
(nodding off again)
Go back to sleep, kid. You're dreaming.

ESCAPEE
No ... I couldn't be.
(talking to the sky)
Just tell me where to go. Just tell me where ...

INT. LIZ'S LIVING ROOM - THE DEAD OF NIGHT

Nancy tosses and turns on the couch, knocking over the empty champagne bottle.

INT. LIZ'S BEDROOM

Liz tosses and turns, too, groaning and scratching in her sleep.

INT. SAL AND PHYLLIS'S BEDROOM

Sal and Phyllis, lying together like spoons, are sleeping peacefully.

EXT. THE AMAZON'S PLANET (JUNE'S DREAM) - DAY

(NOTE: The MUSIC accompanying this dream -- and possibly the three previous scenes, too -- is an instrumental version of "OVER THE RAINBOW.")

June is walking by a stream that runs alongside a lush green field. She wears a white Grecian tunic and has flowers in her hair.

The Amazon, similarly dressed and with a purple cloak across her shoulders, joins June on the bank. They kiss. The MUSIC SWELLS.

CUT TO:

INT. JUNE AND NANCY'S BEDROOM - MORNING

June wakes from her dream with the Amazon gone. She panics.

> JUNE
> Dawn! Dawn!

The Amazon rushes in, naked and dripping wet again, and joins her on the bed. She holds June and gets her wet.

> AMAZON
> Sorry – I'm dripping.

> JUNE
> That's all right.
> (leaning back)
> Oh, Dawn – I was in a place that was so beautiful and so real – and you were there, too. But you couldn't have been, could you?
> (startled)
> My God, I sound like Judy Garland.

INT. LIZ'S LIVING ROOM

The morning paper HITS the front door and Nancy wakes up stiff on the couch. She gets up, stretching painfully, and accidentally kicks the champagne bottle with her bare foot.

> NANCY
> Ow!

Amazon X   185

She hobbles around the room and over to the door. When she opens the door, the big bunch of lavender balloons (which has been tied to the doorknob all night long) floats inside. Nancy has to stoop under it to reach the paper, which she picks up and brings inside.

INSERT OF THE PAPER

revealing the Escapee's picture on the front page with the headline "WHERE IS SHE NOW?"

BACK TO SCENE

Nancy sees the picture and automatically assumes it's the Amazon.

NANCY
(continuing)
Oh my God – it *is* her! Junie!

She grabs her pants and puts them on, shouting to Liz in the bedroom.

NANCY
(continuing)
I have to go – emergency!   I'll – I'll – I don't know – I'll call you . . .

Half-dressed, carrying her shirt and shoes, she runs out the door, fighting her way through the balloons and leaving the door open. Liz comes out of the bedroom, talking to Nancy.

LIZ
What? Darling? I'm all better.

Then she sees the balloons and runs screaming back into the bedroom, SLAMMING the DOOR.

EXT. GREYHOUND BUS STATION - CLOSEUP - NEWSPAPERS

There's an uncut bundle of newspapers sitting on the sidewalk, with the Escapee's picture on the front page.

IN FRONT OF THE STATION

Mary and the Escapee stop beside the bundle of newspapers.

MARY
Say, is this where you're bringing me? Their eggs are so greasy they slide right in your lap.

ESCAPEE
I better not go in. Here, Mary –

She hands over the money Mary gave her yesterday.

ESCAPEE
(continuing)
– get yourself a one-way ticket to Florida.

MARY

Yeah? And what're you gonna do?

ESCAPEE

I'm going somewhere else ... I hope.

Mary tries to give the money back.

MARY

Then you're gonna need this.

ESCAPEE

No – and I won't need this, either.

She takes the gun out of her pocket and puts it in her garbage bag. She pulls off her wool cap, puts it in, too, and sticks the whole bag in a wire trash barrel.

ESCAPEE

Good luck, Mary.

She gives Mary a hug. Mary pretends not to like it. In the b.g. a POLICEMAN is watching them both.

MARY

Ah, mush – cut it out – go on, get outta here.

The Escapee turns to leave and sees the Policeman, who is on the verge of recognizing her. She freezes with fear. Mary sees the cop, too, and gives her a shove.

MARY
(continuing; under her breath)

Go – quick –

The Escapee breaks and runs. The Policeman starts to go after her and Mary grabs him tightly and goes limp, dragging him down with her and screaming at the top of her lungs.

MARY
(continuing)

AHH, MY HEART – MY HEART – GET A DOCTOR, GET A PRIEST, GET A WAGON FULL OF NUNS – I'M A GONER!

The Policeman works himself free of Mary and runs in the direction of the Escapee.

CLOSE SHOT - MARY

Mary leans up on one elbow and watches him chasing the Escapee.

MARY
(continuing)

Good luck, kiddo.

INT. JUNE AND NANCY'S KITCHEN

June in her bathrobe is having coffee. The Amazon is dressed and standing by the open back door. She is hoping the Escapee will show up any minute.

                              JUNE
          Would you – like a cup of wine?
                              (beat)
          Or breakfast – maybe a microwave lasagna?

                              AMAZON
                              (preoccupied)
          No, thank you.

                              JUNE
          Are you waiting on someone?

                              AMAZON
          Yes.

                              JUNE
          Will they be here soon?

                              AMAZON
          I hope so.

The Amazon realizes it sounds like she's eager to go. She leaves her post to take June in her arms.

                              AMAZON
                              (continuing)
          I'm sorry I have to leave now.

                              JUNE
          Oh, so am I . . . but I'm glad you picked my garbage to land in.

                              AMAZON
          It's a great honor, June Foster – not to land in your garbage, but
          to know you. You're so brave and beautiful –

                              JUNE
                              (embarrassed)
          Oh, please . . .

                              AMAZON
          I mean it. To live in such a world as this takes great courage.
          To try and make things better must take even more.

                              JUNE
          I've got to believe there's something better. I don't have a choice.

                              AMAZON
          Ah, but you do. Always.

                              JUNE
          Well . . .

She kisses the Amazon. Then she has one more question.

> **JUNE**
> (continuing)
> I don't suppose you could take me with you?

> **AMAZON**
> I wish ... I'm sorry.

> **JUNE**
> Oh, it was just a thought.

> **AMAZON**
> You're needed here.

> **JUNE**
> You mean that's why? Not because it's not allowed or I wouldn't fit in or you don't love me?

> **AMAZON**
> None of those things.
> (beat)
> If you were hurt and in trouble and had nowhere left to go, then I would take you. But if you were, you wouldn't be you, and I might not love you this way ... and I do love you ... very much.

They kiss again. June makes one last suggestion.

> **JUNE**
> You know, if you'll give me a minute, I'm sure I can get in some kind of trouble.

There's a KNOCK at the front door.

> **JUNE**
> (continuing)
> Maybe I already am ... I'll have to get that.

She reluctantly goes toward the front door. The Amazon pauses a moment and then walks out into the backyard.

EXT. DORIS AND BETTY'S BACKYARD - THE DECK

Doris and Betty are sitting on their deck with coffee and the paper. Doris studies the picture of the Escapee.

> **DORIS**
> Sure looks like her to me.

> **BETTY**
> Look ...

Doris and Betty watch the Amazon cross the backyard and peer into the alley. Doris looks from the Amazon to the picture and back.

> **DORIS**
> But there's something different about the eyes ... up close, I mean.

BETTY
You can't always tell from a photograph.

EXT. JUNE AND NANCY'S BACKYARD

The Amazon looks at her transmitter and up at the sky. Sal and Phyllis come rushing out the back door with June right behind them. Sal has the morning paper in her hand. In the b.g. Doris and Betty are watching.

SAL
There she is!

PHYLLIS
Okay, let's be calm – we can handle this.

JUNE
(to the Amazon)
Uh – look who's here – Dawn, I don't believe you've met Phyllis.

Phyllis holds out her hand, and the Amazon shakes it.

PHYLLIS
(to the Amazon)
Linda, we know who you are, and you have nothing to be afraid of. I'm Phyllis Holder, and I'd like to represent you.

AMAZON
My name is Dawn Brillo.

SAL
We know she's Linda Bradley, June.

JUNE
No, she's not.

Sal shows the paper to June.

PHYLLIS
(to the Amazon)
Believe me, I can help you – I was in the Public Defender's office for five years. Now I know we can deal with these escape charges – stealing the officer's gun may be a little tricky, but you never shot it – you didn't, did you?

AMAZON
(looking at June)
No.

EXT. DORIS AND BETTY'S DECK

Doris and Betty watch Sal, Phyllis, June, and the Amazon talking and gesturing and looking at the paper.

BETTY
Should we call the police?

DORIS
Not on your life. That guy she shot's on my floor – he had three
nurses fetching and carrying all day long – the man's a complete
asshole.
                    (indicating the group)
They'll work it out.

EXT. JUNE AND NANCY'S BACKYARD

The confusion continues.

SAL
                    (to the Amazon)
And I want you to know we still believe what you told us.

PHYLLIS
Absolutely – that hasn't changed – we have faith – in fact, we'll
name her after you.

The Amazon is watching her transmitter and looking into the alley.

AMAZON
That's very nice of you.

JUNE
Sal, Phyl, she's really not from around here –

SAL
June, it's okay.

PHYLLIS
The D.A. owes me a favor, June.

AMAZON
                    (to June)
I'm going to have to leave soon.

JUNE
Oh –
                    (to Sal and Phyllis)
Please, if you'll just –

PHYLLIS
                    (to the Amazon)
Now Linda, you mustn't leave town –

SAL
                    (to the Amazon)
No, no –

JUNE
– go inside I can explain everything –

PHYLLIS
– it would look very bad –

                              SAL
— oh, awful —

                             JUNE
— I need to be alone with her —

                            PHYLIIS
— and I can't predict how another jurisdiction would react.

                              SAL
— don't take the chance, Linda.

                             JUNE
— for just a few minutes, please!

The three women are surrounding the Amazon. Sal and Phyllis are on either side of her and June is in front of her. Suddenly, we HEAR Nancy's voice.

                         NANCY (O.S.)
    Hold it!

All conversation stops.

ANGLE ON NANCY

Nancy stands at the back door. Her hair and dress are disheveled.

EXT. DORIS AND BETTY'S DECK

Doris and Betty see Nancy's arrival.

                            DORIS
    Uh-oh.

EXT. JUNE AND NANCY'S BACKYARD

Nancy comes down the steps and into the yard.

                            NANCY
    Okay — I know what's going on.

June is between Nancy and the Amazon.

                            JUNE
                          (to Nancy)
    This has nothing to do with you.

                           PHYLLIS
                       (to the Amazon)
    Don't say anything.
                          (to Nancy)
    Late night, dear?

                            NANCY
    I've seen the paper.

SAL
(to Nancy)
So have we – that's why we're here.

June snatches Sal's paper.

JUNE
This is ridiculous – Dawn has no connection to this woman.

AMAZON
(correcting her)
Yes, I do – I've called her, and she's coming.

JUNE
(surprised)

Oh.

SAL

Who's coming?

PHYLLIS
What is this – multiple personality?

AMAZON
But she'll have to be here very soon.

JUNE
(to the Amazon)
Couldn't we go inside and say good-bye?

The Amazon shakes her head gently.

PHYLLIS
(thinking of her case)
Ooh, insanity plea – this could be complicated.

SAL
Phyl, she can't be crazy – she's our godmother.

NANCY
Look – I don't care about any of this. You handle it, Phyl, just
leave June out of it.

PHYLLIS

That won't be so easy.

NANCY

June – we need to talk.

JUNE
(to Nancy)

We can talk later.

(to all except the Amazon)
Will you all please go inside and leave us alone for a minute?

NANCY

All right, I don't care who hears me – I'm sorry.

(beat)

June, I'm sorry.

Amazon X   193

Everybody looks at Nancy.

> **NANCY**
> (continuing)
> I've lied to you, I've cheated on you, and I'm very, very sorry. This is all my fault —

> **JUNE**
> No, it isn't.

> **NANCY**
> — if I'd been there for you, you wouldn't have gotten mixed up in this.
> (to the Amazon)
> But you were right — I should never have lied. It was all a stupid game — and I'm sorry.
> (to June)
> Please forgive me.

> **JUNE**
> (also confessing)
> I slept with Dawn last night.

> **NANCY**
> It's all right.

> **JUNE**
> I know it is. And now I'm going to say good-bye to her.

June turns and kisses the Amazon in front of everybody.

EXT. DORIS AND BETTY'S DECK

Doris and Betty watch June kissing the Amazon.

> **DORIS**
> Boy — this is almost as good as a movie.

> **BETTY**
> Better.

EXT. JUNE AND NANCY'S BACKYARD

June and the Amazon continue kissing. Sal asks Phyllis and Nancy a question about the Amazon.

> **SAL**
> I don't understand — where is she going?

> **PHYLLIS**
> (to Nancy)
> I hope this won't color your judgment of the case.

> **NANCY**
> I deserve it. Phyl, if she wants to leave, let her go.

But she'll never make it ...

TWO SHOT - JUNE AND THE AMAZON

June and the Amazon stop kissing. They talk quietly.

JUNE

Will you ever come back?

AMAZON

I hope so ... but you mustn't wait for me.
(beat)
Nancy does love you.

JUNE

I know.

She gives the Amazon a final embrace.

JUNE
(continuing)
I wish I were going --
(indicating the others)
-- I wish we all were.

AMAZON
(touching June's face)
You're already there --
(touching her own chest)
-- in your hearts.

THE BACKYARD - FULL SHOT

The Amazon steps back and adjusts her transmitter. She takes one more
look down the alley.

AMAZON
(continuing)
I guess she isn't coming.
(to Phyllis)
Do what you can to help her.

PHYLLIS

I want to help *you*, if you'll let me.

SAL

Please don't go.

NANCY

June ...

JUNE

Good-bye, Dawn.

Good-bye, June Foster.
                    (holding up her hand)
Love.

The Amazon vanishes into thin air.

CLOSE SHOT - JUNE

June looks up in the sky as the others gasp.

EXT. DORIS AND BETTY'S DECK

They saw the Amazon disappear, too.

                    DORIS
Betty?

                    BETTY
I saw it.

                    DORIS
Oh, good. I thought I needed a new prescription.

Doris takes off her glasses to polish them.

                    BETTY
Do people just disappear like that now?

                    DORIS
These days? All the time.

                    BETTY
You better not.

                    DORIS
Honey, I'm not going anywhere.

EXT. JUNE AND NANCY'S BACKYARD

June is waving at the sky and smiling wistfully. Everyone else is in shock.

                    JUNE
                (saying good-bye)
Love.

                    PHYLLIS
Where did she go?

Sal is holding her stomach. Now she really believes.

                    SAL
I'm having a baby ...

                    NANCY
Then she really was – that's how she knew all those – oh my
God ...

The Escapee bursts out of the alley, frightened and gasping for breath. They all look at her.

ESCAPEE

Am I too late?

NANCY

Who are you?

ESCAPEE

Linda Bradley.

SAL
(comparing her to the Amazon)
Why, they're really very different, aren't they?

JUNE
(answering the Escapee)
I'm sorry – she just left.

PHYLLIS
(starting over)
Linda, it's all right. I'm an attorney – I can help you.

The Escapee looks up, pleading.

ESCAPEE
(to the sky)
Please take me.

And as Phyllis reaches out a hand in friendship, the Escapee also disappears.

PHYLLIS
(jumping)
Whoa! Was it something I said?

JUNE

People come and go so quickly here.

SAL
(almost to herself)
They were so different.

JUNE
(agreeing with Sal)
It's all in where you come from ... and where you're going.

NANCY
(hesitantly)

June?

June looks at Nancy -- then at Sal and Phyllis, too. She smiles.

JUNE

Would anyone like some breakfast? There's plenty of spaghetti ...

EXT. DORIS AND BETTY'S DECK

They watch as June takes Nancy's hand to go inside -- maybe the two of them will work things out. Sal and Phyllis follow, with Sal still holding her stomach and excitedly showing Phyllis how it'll expand with the baby.

BETTY
Now – how did she do that twice?

DORIS
That was someone else.

BETTY
I must need *my* prescription changed.

June and Nancy's backyard is empty. Doris goes back to reading the paper. There's a loud GARBAGE CAN RATTLE, and Betty looks over the railing.

BETTY
(continuing)
Why, somebody took our garbage.

DORIS
Cans, too?

BETTY
Nope – just the garbage.

DORIS
(shrugging)
They're welcome to it.

She sees an article in the paper.

DORIS
(continuing)
Did you see this about those guys they found frozen in that alley downtown? Says all they can do is blink.

Betty leans over to read over Doris's shoulder. The VOICEOVER of a final news item comes UP as we

DISSOLVE TO:

A BLACK SCREEN

ANNOUNCER (V.O.)
– and Commissioner Kelly announced police have now called off their statewide search, saying "it's almost as if she's vanished off the face of the earth."

We HEAR a synthesized space version of "MY LITTLE CORNER OF THE WORLD" as the CREDITS RUN. It PLAYS all the way through to:

FADE OUT.

THE END